DIFFERENCE: AN AVOIDED TOPIC IN PRACTICE

THE LONDON CENTRE FOR PSYCHOTHERAPY

PRACTICE OF PSYCHOTHERAPY SERIES

Series Editors

Bernardine Bishop, Angela Foster,
Josephine Klein, Victoria O'Connell

Book One: Challenges to Practice
Book Two: Ideas in Practice
Book Three: Elusive Elements in Practice

PRACTICE OF PSYCHOTHERAPY SERIES

BOOK FOUR

DIFFERENCE: AN AVOIDED TOPIC IN PRACTICE

edited by
*Angela Foster, Adrian Dickinson,
Bernardine Bishop, Josephine Klein*

on behalf of
The London Centre for Psychotherapy

Routledge
Taylor & Francis Group
LONDON AND NEW YORK

First published 2006 by Karnac Books Ltd.

Published 2018 by Routledge
2 Park Square, Milton Park, Abingdon, Oxon OX14 4RN
711 Third Avenue, New York, NY 10017, USA

Routledge is an imprint of the Taylor & Francis Group, an informa business

British Library Cataloguing in Publication Data

A C.I.P. record for this book is available from the British Library

ISBN13: 9781855759732 (pbk)

Edited, designed, and typeset by RefineCatch Ltd, Bungay, Suffolk

CONTENTS

EDITORS AND CONTRIBUTORS

BERNARDINE BISHOP has a background in academic English, writing and teaching. She is a psychoanalytic psychotherapist in private practice in London, and is a Full Member of the London Centre for Psychotherapy (LCP) and of the Lincoln Centre.

PROPHECY COLES is a psychoanalytic psychotherapist. She is the author of *The Importance of Sibling Relationships in Psychoanalysis* (Karnac, 2003) and she has recently edited *On Sibling Relationships*, to be published by Karnac in 2006.

MARIE CONYERS has worked in private practice for 15 years. She writes, lectures and trains medical and paramedical staff on aspects of mental health. She qualified from the LCP in 1993, and is also an accredited Member of the British Association of Counselling and Psychotherapists (Senior Practitioner). She has undertaken extensive research and published several articles and a book on aiding emotional adjustment to visual impairment and disability.

DOROTHY DANIELL trained at the LCP and qualified in 1981, becoming a Full Member in 1985. Since then she has maintained a full private practice, and been involved in many areas of the life of the LCP. For the past three years she has also been working at the Refugee Therapy Centre, now at 40 St Johns Way, London N19 3RR. As her chapter describes, she has become intensely interested in the interface between the political, personal and practical problems with which refugees contend, and the special contribution which psychotherapy can offer.

ADRIAN DICKINSON is a Full Member of the London Centre for Psychotherapy, having qualified in 1990, and has a private practice in London. He taught English Literature at various independent schools for 28 years and has given talks and conducted seminars on his particular interest, the English Romantic poets as precursors of psychoanalytic thinking, for the LCP, the C.G. Jung Analytical Psychology Club, the Forum for Independent Psychotherapists, and the London Bi-Logic Group.

ANGELA FOSTER is a psychoanalytic psychotherapist in private practice and a founding member of FRC Consultants providing psychoanalytic and systemic consultancy and professional development services to organizations and individuals. She has published widely in the field of mental health and is co-editor and a principal contributor to *Managing Mental Health in the Community: Chaos and Containment*, (Foster A. & Roberts V. Z. (Eds.), Routledge, 1998).

SUE GOTTLIEB is a psychoanalytic psychotherapist in private practice in Somerset. Her background is in neurophysiology. She teaches for the Severnside Institute for Psychotherapy and lectures at Bristol University. She is the author of "The capacity for love" published in *Love and Hate: Psychoanalytic Perspectives*, D. Mann (Ed.), Brunner-Routledge, 2002, and various papers.

JOSEPHINE KLEIN was an academic for the first 20 years of her professional life and then a psychoanalytic psychotherapist, now retired. She has written *Our Need for Others and its Roots in Infancy* (Routledge, previously Tavistock, 1987), *Doubts and Uncertainties in the Practice of Psychotherapy* (Karnac Books, 1995), and *Jacob's Ladder; Essays on Experiences of the Ineffable in the Context of Psychotherapy* (Karnac Books, 2003).

FRANK LOWE has a background in psychology and social work. He trained as a Psychotherapist at the LCP and qualified in 1999. He has been a senior manager in social services responsible for children and adult mental health services and currently works as a Social Services Inspector with the Commission for Social Care Inspection and as a Psychotherapist and Senior Clinical Lecturer in Social Work at the Tavistock Clinic.

STEVEN MENDOZA was a postgraduate student of Human Learning at Brunel University and a generic social worker. He has been a teacher for the LCP and other trainings and has worked full time in private practice since 1982. He is the author of "Genital and phallic homosexuality" published in *Sexuality: Psychoanalytic Perspectives* (Harding, C. (Ed.). Brunner-Routledge, 2001).

RICHARD MORGAN-JONES practises post-freudian psychoanalysis as a psychotherapist in Sussex on the south coast of the UK. He is a Full Member, training therapist and training supervisor of the LCP. He also works as an organizational consultant offering human systems analysis and transformational change. He is co-director of the Work Force Health Consortium in association with Sussex University. He is a member of the Organisation for Promoting Understanding of Society (OPUS) and the Forum International de l'Innovation Sociale (FIIS/IFSI-Paris). He has published articles about consultancy work and edited a book that surveys psychotherapy trainings within the analytic tradition, entitled *Psycho/analytic Psychotherapy Trainings: A Guide.*

ELIZABETH REDDISH worked for 15 years in the film industry reaching the post of Head of European Distribution for the British Film Institute after graduating in linguistics from York University. She qualified as a psychoanalytic psychotherapist in 1996 and although she principally works in private practice, she recently spent a year working in the Crisis Intervention Service at the Royal London Hospital. She has published two articles on psychoanalytic perspectives on film in the *British Journal of Psychotherapy.*

JENNIFER SILVERSTONE is a training therapist and supervisor for the LCP. She has written on Benjamin Wilkomirski and is interested in truth and fiction and its relationship to literature and psychoanalysis.

The London Centre for Psychotherapy

The London Centre for Psychotherapy has its origins in the 1950s and became a registered charity in 1974. Its activities are threefold:

- to offer training in psychoanalytic psychotherapy (including analytical psychology) in which the leading schools of analytic thought and practice are represented;
- to organise post-graduate professional activities, and;
- to provide a psychotherapy service to the community through its clinic.

The Centre is the professional association of around 200 practising psychotherapists who are registered, through the Centre, with the British Psychoanalytic Council.

The LCP

32 Leighton Road ● Kentish Town ● London NW5 2QE
Telephone: 020 7482 2002/2282 ● Fax: 020 7482 4222

www.lcp-psychotherapy.org.uk

Registered Charity No. 267244

Introduction

Angela Foster

D ifference is a complex and often disturbing issue. Taking the lead from Chapter One, the purpose of this book is "to encourage a culture of open enquiry into an emotionally charged subject" (see p. 5) which, the editors argue, has been largely avoided by the profession.

> Theoretically . . . psychoanalysis is all about recognition and appreciation of difference, yet the psychoanalytic profession itself does not have a good reputation in this area. We are often accused of being blind to difference, choosing only to work with people who are willing and able to work with us in the way we deem fit. [See Chapter One, page 6].

This is a courageous collection. Each author has been prepared to go into print about situations in which difference is a significant element in the work and one around which they have felt uneasy and uncertain as they found themselves in uncharted territory for which their training left them ill-prepared. Lacking adequate maps in the mind each contributor analyses their experience and that of their patients and clients in order to arrive at new understandings

1

and insights. Taking this metaphor further we hope that this book will help and encourage others to do the same and provide some useful new maps for future reference. Differences matter and specific issues that alert us to difference serve as a reminder that difference is always present in the consulting room.

In Chapter One, taking the view that "failure to explore difference is tantamount to bad psychotherapy", Angela Foster writes about the often violent and shame-inducing unconscious emotional processes that operate around difference in our consulting rooms, on training courses and in organizations. She invites the reader to reflect on how these processes might operate within their own places of work and offers suggestions as to how one might intervene effectively to tackle these destructive dynamics.

In Chapter Two Dorothy Daniell provides a valuable illustration of the experience of a therapist who is prepared to join her asylum-seeking clients in venturing into the unknown, learning together about the terrain which is new for all of them and finding a way of finding each other within it.

> Choosing to work with refugees opens a door onto a world which is vast and unknown. The differences of race, culture, language and experience which they bring meet all the cross-currents of projection and expectation. The impact of difference is great. [p. 26]

In Chapter Three Frank Lowe explores the struggle for the profession as a whole to find ways of thinking and working that incorporate racial difference effectively, by addressing and overcoming the inherent institutionalized racism that is embedded in early psychoanalytic writing as well as in our own cultural makeup.

> This chapter highlights the failure of psychoanalysis to face its own truths about issues of race and white racism in the selection and training of psychotherapists and in the delivery of psychotherapy. It explores possible reasons for this failure and calls for action to make psychotherapy less racially exclusive and more responsive to the needs of a multi-racial and multi-cultural society. [p. 43]

Chapter Four is a collection of pieces in which therapists write about their experiences of dealing with situations requiring a deviation from conventional professional practice. Each highlights how the therapists concerned improvised when finding themselves in uncharted territory, the challenge being "How to proceed without falling down and injuring ourselves, our patients or the reputation of our profession?"

Some of these situations are becoming increasingly common. For example, as patterns of work in our society change, we might all come across patients who are required to work elsewhere for periods of time. Elizabeth Reddish shares her experience of continuing her work via telephone calls with her patient. Other situations, such as the need to pick up and look after the patients of a suddenly dead colleague, are unexpected and always distressing. This is sensitively explored by Prophecy Coles. Then there is the matter of negotiating one's own retirement which Josephine Klein describes in a manner that can be of use to us all. Jennifer Silverstone ends this chapter with a piece entitled "Staying well" in which she identifies the responsibilities therapists have for their own mental and physical health and that of their colleagues.

This theme is developed in the next two chapters, both focusing on differences brought into the consulting room by the therapist, through pregnancy (Chapter Five) and disability (Chapter Six). These can be thought of as unwanted intrusions into the patient's therapeutic space. While we might be more experienced in addressing unwanted intrusions from the wider environment – doorbells ringing or background family noise – these differences come right into the consulting room as changes in the person of the therapist.

In Chapter Five Sue Gottlieb writes "The emotions and ideas evoked by pregnancy might be normal grist for the analytic mill were it not for the fact that the therapist's pregnancy itself constitutes such an intrusion into the analytic setting as it has been established" (p. 8). Then in Chapter Six Marie Conyers describes how difficult and painful as well as how useful it can prove to be if disability is overtly present in the consulting room. In these detailed papers both authors consider when and what to tell their patients, the impact of the intrusion into the therapeutic space, its transference meaning and the outcome for their patients.

In Chapter Seven Steven Mendoza takes us back to something more familiar, focusing on the extremely complex and relatively unexplored difference between the one who pays and the one who is paid: "We may feel unhappy about charging if we have not analysed properly the feeling that we give nothing of value. Of course the denial can always take the manic form of a greedy insistence on the inflated value of our work and the refusal to be self-critical" (p. 119). From the patient's point of view how is love to be paid for and if there is a fee how is it set and how is it experienced?

Finally in Chapter Eight Richard Morgan-Jones highlights another difference that requires adaptations in technique – the dangerous patient. Describing his role in providing supervision for staff working in a forensic unit he identifies the emotional impact of the work. This links back to Chapter One as he recognizes the need for a form of supervision that is robust enough to contain the disturbance, providing the staff with an opportunity to process their experiences and increase their understanding of their patients thereby limiting the risk of destructive re-enactment of the patients' earlier traumas.

Richard Morgan-Jones uses a phrase of Bion's, "The experienced officer is one who can think while under fire" (Bion, 1986, p. 130) that aptly sums up a theme running throughout this book. All contributors describe times when, finding themselves in unfamiliar territory, such thinking has been particularly difficult, even impossible to achieve. Then, through painstaking analysis of their experience, each provides the reader with some useful insights and guidelines for future reference as well as some clear and stimulating illustrations of effective thinking in strange and disturbing situations. What makes this thinking effective is the demonstrated ability of all contributors to preserve their analytic functioning whatever the circumstances.

CHAPTER ONE

Living and working with difference and diversity

Angela Foster

Introduction

The aim of this chapter is to encourage a culture of open enquiry into an emotionally charged subject, drawing on my experiences as a psychoanalytic psychotherapist in private practice, as an organizational consultant working mainly in mental health and child care services and as a teacher delivering a syllabus entitled "Living and working with difference and diversity" to students of psychoanalytic approaches to organizational consultancy. Taking the view that failure to explore difference is tantamount to bad psychotherapy I use psychoanalytic theory to identify those dynamics at individual, group and organizational levels that make good work in the area of difference so hard to achieve, whether in the consulting room, the classroom or the workplace. I refer specifically to issues of ethnicity, class, gender and sexuality, though the psychological processes identified would apply to other areas of difference.

I identify ways of facilitating discussions on difference and discuss ways of creating and preserving adequate containers for this work, touching on the fact that this is complicated by the dynamics of postmodern organizations, post 9/11 paranoid anxiety and a societal culture of narcissism. Finally, I identify a set of conditions which help to make this work possible.

Difference in psychoanalysis

Theoretically we could argue that psychoanalysis is all about recognition and appreciation of difference, yet the psychoanalytic profession itself does not have a good reputation in this area. We are often accused of being blind to difference, choosing only to work with people who are willing and able to work with us in the way we deem fit. Our institutions, largely made up of therapists, trainees and patients, are full of white middle-class people, something that is particularly striking in London where the resident community, unlike the psychoanalytic community, is so mixed both racially and culturally.

Are we, in the psychoanalytic profession, guilty of complacency, taking what is often construed as a superior position in preference to struggling with what is unfamiliar and therefore makes us uncomfortable? What is it that we should be doing in order to work well with people who, through their life experience, might be highly sensitive to anything which could be construed as criticism from on high or who might view our approach as weird and irrelevant because they are not used to working in our preferred way, don't see the sense in it and therefore wouldn't choose it? How can we find ways of communicating effectively to a wider range of people without compromising our professional integrity?

Defining difference

Kleinian psychoanalytic thinking on difference falls into two areas, Pre-Oedipal, narcissistic, paranoid-schizoid functioning and Post-Oedipal, depressive position functioning, which is reached through successful negotiation of the Oedipus complex. In paranoid-schizoid mode we use splitting and projection to rid ourselves of those aspects of our personalities we dislike, locating them in others, whom we then denigrate. We operate in terms of bi-polar judgements and relationships – everything is either good or bad and people are identified as "with me or against me", "one of us or one of them". There is no middle ground and no room for thoughtful debate of complex relationships and situations. This is a narcissistic mental state in which difference is either hated and or denied, where the focus is on the self, and dependence on others is defended against.

When we can recognize and contain these narcissistic traits, holding in mind both the good and the bad, it shows our ability to negotiate Oedipal dynamics. In developmental terms this occurs as children begin to acknowledge that their parents are different from each other, have a relationship that excludes them and are capable of things that little people cannot do. Thus in this mode we are acknowledging difference not only in kind but also in power. If acknowledging difference meant that we would all be equal the task would be much easier than it is. All this arouses a range of uncomfortable feelings which have to be managed and contained if we are to function in depressive position mode. These feelings are:

- loss of the fantasized exclusive relationships between parent and child,
- envy of the parents and their relationship,
- shame at being lacking, needy and dependent, and
- guilt about now owned, but previously projected, bad parts.

We hope that in psychoanalysis and in life we become more able to bear these feelings thus increasing our capacity for depressive position functioning and our ability to locate what Britton (1989) refers to as the third position.

> If the link between the parents perceived in love and hate can be tolerated in the child's mind, it provides him with a prototype for an object relationship of a third kind in which he is a witness and not a participant. A third position then comes into existence from which object relationships can be observed. Given this, we can also envisage *being* observed. This provides us with a capacity for seeing ourselves in interaction with others and for entertaining another point of view whilst retaining our own, for reflecting on ourselves whilst being ourselves. [Britton, 1989, p. 87]

This enables us to struggle with and to think about confusing and disturbing situations. However, in times of anxiety and stress we unconsciously resort to the false security of Pre-Oedipal functioning. In the next section I bring together quotes from a range of authors to illustrate how these dynamics operate intra-psychically and socially and what it is like to be on the receiving end of them.

Pre-Oedipal dynamics in everyday life

Meltzer (1992) describes how a desire for comfort can lead to a "delusion of clarity of insight . . . 'sitting in judgement' . . . smugness, superciliousness, aloofness and pride" (p.75). He is illustrating what he calls the claustrum, a paranoid internal world akin to a gang culture in which one feels bullied into submission and conformity because to dissent would lead to exposure, humiliation and banishment. He continues,

> One way or other, the outcome is degradation, not only, of course, in behaviour but more essentially . . . in the ability to think as a basis for action. [pp. 91–92]

Rustin (1991) describes racism as a product of the same kind of psychic process thus linking internal dynamics with social behaviour.

> The mechanisms of psychotic thought find in racial categorizations an ideal container. These mechanisms include the paranoid splitting of objects into the loved and the hated, the suffusion of thinking processes by intense, unrecognized emotion, confusion between self and object due to the splitting of the self and massive projective identification, and hatred of reality and truth . . . The emptiness of racial categories renders them particularly good vehicles for pseudo-thinking, and for what Bion calls lies – that is, pseudo-thinking intended to defend against the apprehension of reality. [Rustin, 1991, pp. 62–63]

Being on the receiving end

To be black in a white world is agony. This is because the white world as we know it is racist, which means that, if you are black, you are not readily allowed to be yourself. At every turn you are confronted by the practical operation of powerful stereotypes that push you into acting, thinking and feeling in particular ways. At best you feel under pressure either to fit in with such expectations, or to react against them. This pressure makes it exceptionally difficult to keep hold of what you yourself think, feel or want; it is a struggle to keep sane. [Davids, 1992, p. 19]

Note the similarities between this quote and the following which describes the experience of a working-class scholarship girl in a grammar school. She is keen to learn, abides by the rules and produces work of a good standard but,

Because the school's social class values were so ingrained, it was impossible to give a name to my own feeling of not belonging. If certain things about being at school felt uncomfortable, the problem, I thought, must lie with me. It was surely my own fault if I did not fit in . . . teachers and fellow pupils behaved with a niceness that can only be described as relentless: it had a cool, detached, numbing quality that left you feeling as if you did not quite exist. I knew very well that I was not one of them . . . and that my difference was something to be ashamed of. I soon learned to keep as much of myself and my life hidden from view, staying quiet about things that really mattered. [Kuhn, 1995, p. 88]

You can so easily internalise judgements of a different culture and believe – no, *know* – that there is something shameful and wrong about you, that you are inarticulate and stupid, have nothing to say of any value or importance, that no-one will listen to you in any case, that you are undeserving, unentitled, cannot think properly, are incapable of "getting it right". You know that if you pretend to be something else, if you try to act as if you were one of the entitled, you risk exposure and humiliation. And you learn that these feelings may return to haunt you for the rest of your life. [Kuhn, 1995, pp. 97–98]

Margaret Drabble's semi-autobiographical novel *The Peppered Moth* (2000), provides us with an account of a woman haunted. Bessie, whose experience was not unlike Kuhn's, was embittered, rendering not only her life a misery but also those of her husband and children especially her daughter, thus indicating how the impact of these experiences can be passed on to future generations. Dickinson (2001) concludes that "There is something bleakly admirable in Bessie's refusal to compromise" because she could not have achieved the success that would have given her satisfaction. She was "oppressed by a veil of class and gender".

Davids (1998) identifies these dynamics as an internal racist organization, a form of psychic retreat which is extremely resistant to change precisely because it provides refuge from both paranoid and depressive anxieties.

> Each and every one of us has an internal racist in a corner of our mind, and in our professional encounter with someone from a different cultural/ethnic background it is unconscious guilt associated with internal racism that paralyses our functioning. The components are
>
> - "The perception of an attribute on which subject and object differ. Although most visible, skin colour is not the only attribute used for this purpose. Language dialect, geographical origin, class, gender, nationality and many others can all be put to the same use;
> - The use of that difference to project into the object an unwanted/dreaded aspect of the subject's mind, usually something infantile/primitive; and
> - Establishing an organised inner template that governs relations with the object (who now contains the projected parts of the subject). The effect on the victim is that no matter how hard he might try he finds that he is not allowed to be an ordinary human being. This structure functions like a sort of mafia in the mind, promising protection in return for loyalty." [Unpublished paper]

We can hope to reach this internal racist, like any other psychic organization, through our unconscious. When preparing an earlier version of this paper I had a dream in which I was being sacked by a black manager for failing to demand enough from her team. Other black women present made it perfectly clear that they were more forthright in their approach and got better results from the work than I did. I take this as a word of warning about my internal racist and the danger that my need to be accepted could mean that I risk being patronizing and placatory, reinforcing rather than easing anxieties, when faced with cultural and/or racial difference.

At this point I will bring Oedipal dynamics into the discussion while continuing the theme of what it is like to be on the receiving end of an internal racist organization. I wonder if Bessie in Drabble's novel was not only haunted by "a veil of class and gender", but also by a denigration of womanhood such that only success in traditional male terms would have satisfied her. Temperley (1993) notes that

> our extreme dependence on our mothers in infancy and the inequality of power and vulnerability in that relationship can lead both sons and daughters to redress this original imbalance by overvaluing the penis, what the woman does not have. [p. 267]

We might consider that if Bessie had been helped towards a better negotiation of Oedipal dynamics she might have been less haunted and consequently able to locate a more peaceful internal space in which her creativity could have flourished.

> The Kleinian view is that it is not primarily the limiting power of the father that has to be accepted but the reality of our separateness, our dependence on objects we do not control and of our relation to parents whose independent intercourse has to be acknowledged. [Temperley, 1993, p. 274]

Temperley, noting that pre-Oedipal dynamics have confounded thinking about gender, concludes that

> The Oedipus complex is not bad news for women but the possibility both of autonomy and of a sexual relation to men that respects and avails itself creatively of the difference. [p. 273]

Pre-Oedipal thinking has also infused thinking about homosexuality. Zachary (2001) notes that it had been very difficult over the decades to think about homosexuality in a balanced (depressive position) way.

Homosexuality has been classified as a sin, then as a crime, then as an illness. [It has] never quite left the negative environs of these unsatisfactory categories, or of the strong emotions, shame, disgust and anger. [p. 489]

She suggests that,

it is wisest to think of the Oedipus complex as a dynamic concept rather like a lifelong struggle to achieve the elusive depressive position. It is something each individual negotiates internally . . . continually throughout life, occasionally mastering the achievement of real human contact, recognised most poignantly by its loss . . . we need a triangular conceptualisation of perhaps a third space . . . for homosexuals there will always be some sin, some crime and some illness, just as is the case for heterosexuals. The answer lies in keeping things fluid and open-minded, not rigidly set in polarised positions. [p. 492]

Mendoza (2001) similarly suggests that genital love in the depressive position "is a psychology pertaining to the number three and not to gender" (p.163). By this he is referring to the ability to locate the third position in our minds which enables us to engage in mature, loving relationships (p. 163). Sharing the view that this is an ongoing struggle for us all he adds that,

Homosexuals may find the knife edge quality of homosexuality just as ambiguous as others do. They may feel shame about their homosexuality. Even if they do not suffer from the internal persecution which attends the homosexual symptoms of heterosexuals they too are bound to introject the persecutory projections which society directs at them from this widespread shame. [p. 168]

In all these examples it would appear that the people on the receiving end, unlike the perpetrators, experience both paranoid and depressive anxiety. Perhaps most poignantly, when they are experiencing depressive position in-touchness they feel shame about something they have no control over. (They may have their own internal reasons for feeling shame but the shame I am referring to is that which is projected into them and feels like an internal foreign body that the psyche cannot account for.) This happens in consulting rooms, in classrooms and in the workplace.

I will now identify pre-Oedipal dynamics in each of these three settings, highlighting ways of working with these in order to facilitate the shift, if only temporarily, to post-Oedipal depressive position functioning.

The consulting room

It is likely that as therapists we fear the shame we would feel should our internal racist be exposed. This inhibits our ability to empathize and limits our effectiveness in the therapeutic endeavour. Bearing in mind the above examples we must also acknowledge that we may be compounding rather than relieving our patients' distress and we have to ask ourselves whether, through narcissistically charged projective identification, we are subjecting our patients to a kind of claustrum existence? We can appreciate how this might feel because we know from clinical experience what it is like to be coerced by a patient into colluding with a form of pseudo-thinking.

Morgan (1998) writes about shame when working with a black patient, stating

> I didn't actually fear her anger or aggression. More problematic was the possibility of shame at having a racist thought about her. It was the fear of shame that was potentially more debilitating and paralysing. It seems to me that in order that we could work together D and I had to hold two positions simultaneously, of "remembering" that she was black and I was white, and of "forgetting" it. [p. 60]

Jones (2001) describes his struggle in empathizing with his homosexual patient thus:

> In denying myself the acknowledgement of my hatred for him at times, I failed to properly understand his hatred of himself. Similarly his self-disgust and sense of shame eluded me primarily because of my attempts to be fair to him as a reaction to my own fear and anxiety about a homosexual bonding. [p. 501]

However, even when therapists are able to empathize with difference, there are two general aspects of a psychoanalytic approach, identified by Mollon (2002), which, can "if not managed sensitively, significantly evoke shame and thereby impede and distort the therapeutic process" (p. 126). One is the strangeness of the encounter when patients find themselves in a situation when, in a rather Kafkaesque way (described by Davids and Kuhn above), they appreciate that there are rules of behaviour but feel that they will inevitably get them wrong and be found guilty. Secondly, there is the nature of the analyst's interpretation.

> If this is perceived as a quasi-oracular pronouncement which reframes the patient's communications in terms of meanings that were not in any way consciously intended, then inevitably shame will result. [Mollon, 2002, p. 128]

In this way patients' fears are realized. This will mean that some patients leave therapy while others engage in a pseudo-encounter in which their most vulnerable aspects are not revealed.

Here I want to refer to a patient of mine from a different country and culture, who confided in me a shameful family secret which she had been nursing for many years. In spite of her obvious trust in me and her considerable ability to gain insight into the link between her problems and this burden she carried, she decided to take a break in therapy because she felt depleted of the necessary resources to bear the physical and psychological pain of exposing and exploring this. It is possible that I failed to fully appreciate and empathize with the extent of her pain, compounded by a sense of betrayal and shame at making the psychological links and exposing them, and that for this reason the patient will not return. It is also possible that a temporary retreat from therapy may be a healthy short-term option.

In our struggle to think about how we might do better in such situations it is helpful to examine technique in detail. Mollon (2002) describes his approach thus:

> First I try to acknowledge and perhaps articulate the patient's experience from an empathic position. Then, in making interpretations that go beyond the empathic surface, I try to indicate how my idea about what is going on derives from the patient's own communications. In this way my stance is one of trying to understand more of what the patient is trying to tell me, consciously and unconsciously – rather than appearing to present a view of my

own . . . I also try to make my own thought processes explicit so the patient can follow my reasons and inferences. [pp. 134–5]

This, of course also provides the patient with the option of clarifying something misunderstood and of disagreeing with the inferences drawn. Mollon thus hopes to give the patient an experience of

> a fellow human being struggling to use my specialist knowledge to understand . . . and share understanding . . . Finally I try to behave in as "normal" as way as possible while maintaining an analytic stance – giving ordinary vocalisations of understanding, encouragement, and emotional response occasionally. [p. 135]

In general terms, if patients deny difference we view it as a desire to deny dependence and the shame attached to neediness. The challenge for therapists therefore is to address, in our own therapy and development, those aspects of ourselves which are needy – needing attention – and which, if left un-addressed, allow us to turn a blind eye to dynamics that are real and painful for our patients.

The classroom

The earlier quote from Annette Kuhn vividly illustrates *her* experience of the classroom. But this is not uncommon. Students studying difference and diversity have commented on the paralysing anxiety that they experience when the focus of the group is on an obvious area of difference. Does the black person speak on the issue of race or sit back and listen to what others have to say, while simultaneously being aware that the whole group is wondering what s/he will do/ say? Even when the difference is not obvious, anxiety cannot be avoided. Heterosexual students have commented on how challenging and potentially shaming it is to present papers on sexuality, and for homosexual students to declare their own homosexuality to the group requires real courage, though to do so and feel one has the recognition and respect of the group, is liberating.

Bryan and Aymer (1996), two black female teachers of social work, describe the otherness and marginalization of black social work students who, because they are not central to the group, are targets "for projections of badness and madness". These projections become internalized alongside earlier internalizations of shame leading to anxiety about "not being good enough" with the result that they are often openly critical of their experiences on the courses, while secretively feeling gratitude for the training and pride in their achievements (Aymer, 2001). Is it fear of ridicule, humiliation and shame that prevents these successful professionals from having faith in their success and openly celebrating?

As a white woman in authority, I struggled with the sullenness of some black social work students, feeling that they thought I had nothing to offer that would be relevant or valuable to them, and was surprised by their expressions of gratitude on successful completion of their course. I then realized, as presumably they did, that I had given them something valuable by sticking to my task of ensuring that these students, like others, qualified having proved that they were capable of working to the required standard. No one would question that this was indeed my job, but in order to do it I had to overcome my desire to operate in paranoid schizoid mode by either avoiding or attacking these students – to take flight or to fight in response to feeling that I was irrelevant and unwanted. My uncomfortable feelings of being lacking – someone of no value, no interest and no use – can be thought of as feelings these students struggled with which were then located in me, as they had been located in them, via an unconscious process of projective identification. Only by processing this is it possible to arrive at a depressive position response. By seeking out these students in order that we might work together on their professional development I was able to provide the sort of reassurance needed by anyone joining a course with anxieties about "not being the right sort of person" and expectations of "being seen as lacking". However, black students in particular can be badly let down by staff who through fear of shame at their internal racist being exposed and fear of accusations of racism, are inclined to overlook sub-standard work.

This task of acknowledging and exploring difference is further complicated in any professional training group because of the inevitable presence of powerful transferences to the host organization and profession, which often lead one to develop a fantasy of the sort of professional one is supposed to become. One feels pressure to "fit the mould" and a not unrealistic fear that one's work will not pass otherwise. Thus we acquire a new bit of superego that is both persecuting and distracting, and we have to tread a fine line between fitting in and being ourselves in the work. Organizations in the UK now have legal obligations to include different people but are we, particularly in the post 9/11 paranoid climate, in danger of giving out a contradictory, Catch 22 message which essentially says, "you can be different provided you are one of us". Of course, in any training, some degree of "being like us" is required, but how like us someone has to become in order to be one of us is less clear.

Aymer (2001) developed the concept of "co-operative inquiry" groups in which members are encouraged to tell their stories, and through discussion begin to make sense of their experiences.

> Not only did such discussions focus our thinking, but we came to ask ourselves fundamental questions about the nature of black people's psychological development. [Aymer, 2001, p. 132]

Similarly, the Diversity Committee of the London Centre for Psychotherapy also chose to tell their individual stories as a way of beginning to identify and think about issues that the organization might need to address.

Through this process of "co-operative enquiry" in a group of white women with different countries of origin, ethnicity, culture, class and religion, we noted that differences became more bearable as we began to understand each other more fully as individuals, enabling us to recognize and over-ride our stereotypes. We came to view this process as a further resolution of Oedipal dynamics, noting simultaneous developments towards greater intimacy, greater separateness and a sense of aloneness.

We all need to find a way of speaking to our unique experiences but it is difficult to speak and difficult to listen because of the discomfort that accompanies this process. If we acknowledge difference and remain open to understanding it, then we have to be prepared to be influenced and changed by it, with no guarantee that we will like it. When we engage with others we look for similarities; these reassure us and we feel less anxious. We need to find some common ground from which to begin the business of exploring difference. Tools, such as a shared knowledge base like psychoanalytic understanding, help us to reflect on the nature of our discussions as they are happening, thus providing containment for thinking and helping us to strive towards more consistent depressive position functioning in the face of internal and external pressures to retreat to paranoid-schizoid mode. (See Treacher & Foster, 2004 for a more detailed exploration of this material.)

The workplace

Hoggett (1998), acknowledging the contributions of Meltzer, Bion and Rosenfeld, identifies an internal organization in the workplace,

> a highly organized internal agency operating as a kind of gang or Mafia . . . versed in the art of slander and propaganda, which is unleashed at the slightest sign that gang members might desert; the stronger the grip of this organization, the more it resembles a delusional non-human world in which there is both complete painlessness and freedom to indulge in sadistic activity. [pp. 12–13]

People involved in the gang behaviour know it is destructive but are afraid to speak out.

Bion's work on basic assumption groups is relevant here, particularly those defences of One-ness and Me-ness which thrive in narcissistic cultures identified by Turquet (1974) and Lawrence et al. (1996) respectively. Oneness describes group dynamics in which members,

> "seek to join in a powerful union with an omnipotent force" or to be "lost in oceanic feelings of unity". [Turquet, quoted in Cano, p. 84]

> In the case of Me-ness group members defensively collude with "the assumption that there is no group at all – just unaffiliated individuals, whose only joint purpose will be to thwart the formation of a group out of fear that they might be submerged in it or persecuted by it if it did form" [Cano, 1998, p. 84]

Hatcher Cano proposes from her own organizational observations that

> One-ness and Me-ness function alternatively and indifferently, much as fight and flight do . . . where fantasies of total union or total independence take the place of achieving realistic inter-dependence, which is averted or obliterated by attacks on linking. [ibid., p. 92]

These primitive (pre-Oedipal) uses of splitting and projection are recognizable as defences against difference, fear of exposure and shame. It is commonplace these days to hear workers talk openly about their fear of being named and shamed.

In order to perpetuate an illusion of unity, difference has to be avoided and so, paradoxically, each person must work separately. When work is not shared or discussed in meetings, differences in skills and interests cannot be thought about and the very idea of discussing differences in competency is out of the question. Hence bad practice is not addressed and is likely to spread, not least because people become unable to learn from each other. "Cultural narcissism allows the development of a blind eye to perverse and exploitative behaviour" (Long, 2002, p. 187). She refers to evidence of corruption in multi-national companies and "caring institutions" in support of this hypothesis.

This organizational culture is hard to address because it can exist underground for considerable periods of time, emerging most clearly in times of threat, for example when organizational changes are proposed. Times of crisis therefore provide opportunities for constructive intervention, though if they are too frequent, they simply reinforce the hold of the perverse culture. As Long (2002) notes, the lack of traditional forms of containment in post-modern organizations is relevant here. Managers and staff are constantly re-organized around new projects or changes in service delivery. There is an increase in temporary and part-time contracts and in home-based working, and job security is reduced. The organizational focus is increasingly on the individual rather than on the group or the team. This feeds a culture of narcissism in which distrust of management and reluctance to co-operate with management is openly voiced. More secretively, fear of personal impoverishment and anxiety about survival lead to a situation in which the successes of peers are seen as a threat to oneself, and the internal establishment pressures people into hiding their individual talents and operating at the lowest common denominator. Consequently the work lacks thought and creativity and job satisfaction is low.

Effective containment of anxiety is seen as the route to overcoming basic assumption group and organizational anti-task behaviour facilitating a shift, if only temporarily, from the paranoid schizoid mode to task-focused work, in reflective, self-examining, co-operative, depressive mode.

Containment

Work with difference and diversity, with entrenched individual, group and organizational defences operating in post-modern organizations requires a robust container. So what are the necessary components of this? One, indicated earlier, is the need for enough people with a common understanding or purpose and a desire to meet together. This does not have to be everyone nor does it have to operate all the time. This would be an unrealistic expectation (see Foster, 2001). The setting for this work might be a staff support group, team awayday or a large system-wide event such as the one described below.

I was fortunate to have the opportunity of consulting to a large group consisting of the purchasers, the senior management team and the users of a mental health service. In this group the users were able to voice their distress at not being listened to and not respectfully treated within the service. Other members of the group, who had suspected this was the case, were able to hear what was being said and undertook to ensure that respect would be the cornerstone of any service improvements and developments. Needless to say, the main perpetrators of what we might call the perverse culture absented themselves from the event, but it was possible for the senior management team to take this commitment to an awayday in order to plan how changes could be implemented in all areas of the service.

It is not easy to provide the sort of containment necessary to change a culture. The anxiety felt in connection with the initial large group event was such that it had taken the steering committee nine months to plan. Then, in spite of a strong and committed head of service, willing senior managers and purchasers prepared to back the work, I had a struggle to get agreement that disrespectful behaviour must be challenged. Individuals felt afraid of the personal consequences of doing so. It was important for the work that I could appreciate this fear and empathize with what it feels like to be at the mercy of an ever present "internal establishment" recognizing that this could happen to anyone at any time. I could then propose that should anyone of us feel unable to challenge disrespectful behaviour when it occurs, we could and should find a colleague who would take on the task of addressing the matter with the person(s) concerned. It is only through joint agreements to tackle bullying and disrespectful behaviour as it occurs, together with the introduction of measures to support individuals in doing this, that a healthy group culture capable of taking on the perverse culture, can be created.

Work of this kind requires active engagement on behalf of the consultant, and I believe that I am describing a type of organizational consultancy that mirrors Mollon's empathic therapeutic approach, not least because all this work requires us to be sensitive to shame. I certainly felt that I had to "roll up my sleeves" and "get stuck in" perhaps role modelling a way of speaking to the experience and engaging with the contamination of the institutionalized "racist organization", "internal establishment" or "perverse culture", demonstrating a willingness to struggle and a commitment to see it through. This also involved demonstrating what Western (1999) refers to as the need for paternal as well as maternal containment in postmodern organizations.

> The paternal metaphor provides structure, task, boundaries, authority and reality. These are key building blocks helping us to construct a reliable setting in which the containment of anxiety is more likely and a – consultative – space can be created.

> The consultant is not therefore neutral (that is simply a sounding-board or facilitator), but an active partisan who appeals to the "better nature" of both "the group" and the individuals within it. [Hoggett, 1998, p. 23]

The next example demonstrates the use of similar techniques in work where racial and cultural difference predominates. A dedicated multi-ethnic team of workers with the tasks of supporting, teaching and assessing parenting, gave a full, informative presentation of an African refugee family with complex needs and problems exacerbated by the trauma of relocation and the loss of social status they have to bear in this country. As they reported on the mother's apparent refusal to take on certain parenting roles once she was left to do it herself, even though she always said she could and would, the flat tone of the discussion disturbed me. Perhaps the question that could not be posed was whether these children might be removed from their parents because of this seeming impasse. As a way of trying to open up a debate around this, I voiced what I thought was a reality that could not be named. I said it sounded as if they felt they couldn't believe a word the mother said. This rather provocative comment brought the group and the work to life and we began to speculate about the meaning of the mother's evasiveness.

Was it that these tasks were not really her job (too menial?) and that she stood to lose even more status in her marriage and in her community if she did them? Did she actually not realize what was expected of her? Was she lazy? What was her husband's view and just how confused were they about life here and the role of social services as assessors with power not unpaid servants? Was she shamed? Was she depressed? What part did internal racist organizations play in this complex series of encounters and how do we do our jobs in the face of such complex and painful material?

As a way forward in this fraught area of difference and diversity we can strive to stay with the unknown, heeding Bion's (1970, p. 124) advice to analysts to be "aware of those aspects of the material that, however familiar they may seem to be, relate to what is unknown both to him and to the analysand". In order to stay with the unknown Bion advocates that the analyst locates a state of mind he calls "patience", hoping that this term will "retain its association with suffering and tolerance of frustration". "Patience" should be retained without "irritable reaching after fact and reason" until a pattern "evolves" (p. 124). In this space, akin to a transitional space, we have to trust that something is going on internally and inter-personally which will in time enable us to think through our confusion.

Perhaps the boldest attempt at this sort of containment, which aimed at inclusive participation, was the Truth and Reconciliation Commission of South Africa which Haupt and Malcolm (2000) refer to as the provision of a transitional space. A truly post-modern phenomenon, it had an impossible and unbearable task, and when Archbishop Desmond Tutu, the charismatic overseer of both pater-nal and maternal containment, broke down in tears "there appeared to be a sense of relief among staff; a vicarious acknowledgement that the stories were unbearable and the work of witnessing them, demanding in the extreme" (Haupt & Malcolm, 2000, p. 125). The container broke under the strain but this led to a greater acceptance of reality.

> A realisation had been reached that the TRC had limitations; it simply could not take away the pain it was mandated to witness. It could not deliver on the unconscious fantasy of healing the wounds, nor could it deliver a pristine truth or offer reconciliation. [p. 126]

Through this process the container was readjusted and repaired and Haupt and Malcolm conclude that the commission, flawed though it was, provided "a bridge between a hellish past and a hopeful future".

Conclusion

It is those issues which cannot easily be addressed openly that are most likely to be acted out destructively in our consulting rooms, classrooms, organizations or societies. This, whether it is race, class, gender, sexuality or any other area of difference, is to the detriment of all. We need to be vigilant, keeping things under review because as Britton (1998), writes

> the depressive position is no final resting place . . . leaving the security of depressive-position coherence for a new round of fragmented, persecuting uncertainties is necessary for development. [p. 73]

We have to be prepared to experience "psychic discomfort and narcissistic loss", in the hope that we will arrive at new understanding. If we are willing to do this work then others will at least feel that we are prepared to join them in struggling with defensive and destructive behaviour, and in the exploration of new and unknown territory. None of this ever runs smoothly. We need

- a group of people with a shared frame of reference who are willing to meet,
- a desire to address reality however painful,
- a clear structure and task with boundaries and authority,

- an ability to challenge empathically and actively divisive and destructive dynamics located in the individual, the group, the organization or all three,
- sensitivity to shame,
- patience with the process, and finally
- an ability to recognize failures in containment, to name them and work to repair them.

Acknowledgement

With thanks to Fakhry Davids for permission to quote from his unpublished paper.

CHAPTER TWO

A different kind of psychotherapy

Dorothy Daniell

Introduction

I trained as a psychoanalytic psychotherapist, and have many years of experience working with individual patients in a traditional consulting room setting. For the past two years I have been involved in a different kind of psychotherapy at The Refugee Therapy Centre in north London. The chapter that follows describes one of my cases there. It is based on my thoughts, feelings and observations in spending one hour a week with a young refugee couple. They came at first with their 5-month-old baby. During the time I have known them they have had a second baby; the elder child is now two and a half. For reasons of confidentiality I am not describing details of their identity and backgrounds.

I am fortunate to have been able to work with a young woman interpreter from the same culture as the clients. It has been immensely rewarding sharing the experience with her, as will emerge later.

When I am describing work at the Refugee Therapy Centre I shall refer to clients: for work in private practice I shall refer to patients. This corresponds to what is usual in both situations and helps

25

clarification. It is also usual to describe people who are yet without permission to stay here as "asylum seekers". Those who have been granted status are known as "refugees". The family I have been working with are asylum seekers; but I use the term refugees throughout to cover the wider picture.

Choosing to work with refugees opens a door onto a world which is vast and unknown. The differences of race, culture, language and experience which they bring meet all the cross-currents of projection and expectation. The impact of difference is great. Many times I feel, "I wasn't trained to do this!" When patients come for traditional psychotherapy they bring their individual problems of conflict, deficit or trauma. Over time we seem to build up a picture of their inner world and external situation. Private practice brings some sense of security, from our recognized training, a place in society however misunderstood, income and a peer-group network. As every therapist knows, we work often in the dark, often with intractable material, always needing to challenge our own limits of understanding. Yet, in a sense, we do know where we are. The patients have come because of some personal unhappiness or problem they want to resolve. We share a language, and belong to the same British society, roughly recognizable. Patients will probably pay me, and I will listen to their story, picking up transference and countertransference as we go, making such links as may be possible between external and internal, past and present, in the room and out there. Above all, we are grounded in our own therapy or analysis, within a tradition similar to our own practice. As a white, middle-class Englishwoman, what right or qualification do I have to attempt to work with refugees?

There is a need for me to recognize the refugee in myself which draws me to this work. In that the first eight years of my life were spent abroad, I have a personal memory of coming to this country and finding it strange. My parents commuted between two continents: my sense of being geographically rooted in any one place is still tenuous. As a child, I lived with a number of different families: however kind their intentions, their culture felt alien to me. Yet to think of myself as a refugee seems a highly exaggerated statement. I have legal status, preparedness by education for life in this society, all the strength and security of home and personal relationships which remain unthreatened.

Somewhere from my personal history I have a sense of finding a place on the edge of different worlds – looking both ways. The Refugee Therapy Centre is creating its own tradition of training, supervision and practice built on psychodynamic principles, and I am proud to be part of this endeavour. It has a particular purpose and perspective, and a global view of the need for therapy thrown up by the political conflicts and destructiveness of the late twentieth century. I guess that some of my personal involvement in the work comes from survivor guilt at having a secure and comfortable place in a world full of external danger and deprivation. There is also shame at the withdrawal of compassion and humanity in our own society towards refugees, and the massive projection of denigration through misinformation commonly expressed. I feel a need to identify with the outsider, but also to guard against overidentification, which would lead me into a denial of my own privileged position. The work with refugees draws me to a place within myself between the known and the unknown – between the established tradition of psychoanalytic psychotherapy and its development into work with a particular client-need among refugees.

In work with refugees I have found three features of the landscape: confusion, dissociation and the will to survive. The tools of traditional psychoanalytic psychotherapy – transference, countertransference, reliance on the boundaries of the setting, and the attempt to hear the unconscious communication – are to be found in the work: but their use may require adaptation.

Confusion

The couple were originally referred for help with bereavement. They had lost a first baby in tragic circumstances in this country, when the wife was already into her second pregnancy. This would have been hard enough in any event, but for them the pain of loss was made worse by confusion in not understanding what the hospital, the police and the coroner were requiring of them. At the time, they had only a few words of English. The woman became withdrawn and depressed, being tearful much of the time. Her husband took on the role of looking after her and their second baby, when it was born, in a calm and caring way which was genuinely moving. He brought his wife and baby to therapy for her needs, and it was clear he could not begin to think about his own needs. I learned over time that in their culture it is expected that men do not show vulnerability or have emotional need. Before I met them they had had some sessions with a therapist very experienced in this work. She had picked up their bereavement issues confidently, and given them practical suggestions to help them through the grieving process. I was aware that I needed to continue her work. I also assumed that the task was to think about the wider background of trauma which they had experienced in their country of origin, and the hardship they suffered in leaving it.

In fact, the therapeutic time and space, and the therapist's presence, at first seemed to offer little more than some recognizable continuity. My assumption that they would need to talk about the depth of their experience as refugees seemed to conflict with their need to hold on to some sense of present stability, however tenuous. My impression from being with them for a few months was that the massive upheaval and physical and psychical uprooting they had been through created a mental overload, barely containable. Any approach from my side to talk about the bad times seemed to produce a fear of becoming destabilized and unable to function. They seemed to be telling me that they needed to forget, not to remember. I felt grossly inadequate, and turned to any writers I could find who might be helpful: somehow what I was reading about psychoanalytic psychotherapy in work with traumatized patients didn't seem to fit the situation in which I found myself. I put my dilemma of the need to talk about the bad times versus the need to forget to an experienced therapist, who is also Clinical Director of the Centre. She said, "Perhaps they can talk about life in their village before the trauma" (Alayarian, 2002). This simple suggestion became an approach to which they could respond, and for me a first bit of new technique which was appropriate to their needs. They gave me many vivid pictures of the village life they had known, before gradually saying a little about how it had been destroyed. When the husband said, "All is now ruined", it was an accurate description of what had happened in their external world. It was also a description of their internal state in which the known ordering of experience had been overwhelmed: confusion had replaced it. The therapist's experience in this work is that the memory of external trauma can only be approached gradually and in small amounts along with continual holding of present reality. As my supervisor put it, "You take a teaspoon to remove a glacier!" (Thomas, 2003). The need for containment is paramount.

Freud lays down some principles for thinking about trauma. He says in many parts of his writing that trauma is created by any stimulus which overwhelms the mind's ability to deal with it. In *Beyond the Pleasure Principle* he described the mind as having a protective layer to filter excessive stimuli from external sources.

> We describe as "traumatic" any excitations from outside which are powerful enough to break through the protective shield . . . Such an event as an external trauma is bound to provoke a disturbance on a large scale in the functioning of the organism's energy and to set in motion every possible defensive measure. [Freud, 1920, p. 29]

He writes of a danger-situation in *Inhibitions, Symptoms and Anxiety*:

> Clearly it exists in the subject's estimation of his own strength compared to the magnitude of the danger and in his admission of helplessness in the face of it – physical helplessness if the danger is real and psychical helplessness if it is instinctual . . . Let us call a situation of helplessness of this kind that has been actually experienced *a traumatic situation*. [Freud, 1926, p. 166, original emphasis]

He distinguishes clearly between external and internal danger: "A real danger is a danger which threatens a person from an external object, and a neurotic danger is one which threatens him from an instinctual demand" (Freud, 1926, p. 167).

The relationship between the massive external danger which refugees have been exposed to and the impact on their internal state of mind is the crucial question for the therapist attempting to be attuned to them. Freud continues, "the external (real) danger must also have managed to become internalized if it is to be significant for the ego" (1926, p. 168).

In *Introduction to Psychoanalysis and the War Neuroses* (1919), Freud pursues the relationship between the threat of external danger and the threat to the ego of internal change.

> The war neuroses . . . are to be regarded as traumatic neuroses whose occurrence has been made possible or has been promoted by

> a conflict in the ego . . . The conflict is between the soldier's old
> peaceful ego and his new warlike one, and it becomes acute as soon
> as the peace-ego realises what danger it runs of losing its life owing
> to the rashness of its newly formed, parasitic double. [Freud, 1919,
> pp. 208–9]

The refugees I have been with experienced being part of a whole
community that was subjected to terror, and overwhelmed by
external force. They were, like many of the younger generation,
driven to flight. The breaking of contact between the generations
is devastating in a culture where family constellates identity. I
hypothesize that some of the confusion, and absence of ability to
think about the experience they have been through, comes from an
internal disruption in their sense of self, affecting every area of inner
life. Guilt at having left many close friends and relatives behind, and
shame induced by helplessness, are powerful pressures on the ability to maintain a sense of acceptable personal identity. It appears
that the woman was able to maintain a functioning self until the loss
of her baby precipitated her fall into depression. The husband when
I first met him was maintaining himself as her carer, with a cheerful,
courteous demeanour. I was well aware of the cost to him in containing his own anger, pain and loss. In addition, before flight, this gen-
tle man had temporarily been part of resistance fighting. The ability
to go on functioning in the way he is doing at present suggests that
his ego is dealing with internalized trauma "with every possible
defence" in a remarkable way. There is a sense, however, that his life
as a man, vital to his own purposes and identity, is "on hold".

Countertransference

A deeper understanding of psychic reality in the work with the
refugee clients came from my countertransference. (For a long time
there was no transference experience which I could discern apart
from the need for me to be a non-intrusive, reliable, containing presence, part of the institutional framework, which was a kind of matrix.) Sessions were continuing each week; the woman was becoming
less depressed and able to speak a little; the man as ever was
cooperative and caring of his wife. My countertransference was a
feeling of complete impotence and irrelevance, almost futility: also

that there was something different or extra that I should be doing. In other words, I felt oppressed and criticized by my superego. When I was able to understand, quite suddenly one day, that this was exactly what the man felt, it was the beginning of some foothold in the work at a psychic level. I was relieved to be able to pick this up as projective identification, and to be reassured that there was a real engagement in therapy. I was experiencing the husband's sense of impotence and guilt at his flight from his country leaving his parents unprotected. This had been an impossible situation for him, since he was also attracting danger to them. Then he had been unable to avert the personal bereavement which he and his wife had suffered in this country. His only sense of personal validation came from his protective concern for his wife: but this prevented him from speaking about his own pain, and particularly his own sense of guilt and impotence. When I was able to use my countertransference it was possible to find ways to speak to his underlying feeling-state in an empathic way. I also found that this helped me to stay with my own sense of confusion and uncertainty. Confusion and disruption of the kind that I have been describing does not easily translate into words.

With hindsight, I think I began this "different kind of therapy" disguising from myself how great and unfamiliar a challenge it presented. I assumed a kind of pretend normality, as if, being an experienced therapist, I should be familiar with the situation. Yet in many ways it was totally unlike what I had experienced before. For the first time I needed to use an interpreter, and this was an unfamiliar situation for me. She was also new to the work. She was sensitive, helpful and enthusiastic. The man, interpreter and I tried to co-operate to establish a working alliance. The woman remained withdrawn for some months, rarely speaking. In retrospect, it would have been better if I had spent time at the beginning talking about the strangeness of the situation for us all, and perhaps the anxiety we were all feeling.

My response to anxiety was to become much more active than I would usually be in work with patients. Partly this was also realistic and necessary in order to maintain contact across a great divide of cultural difference. On one occasion I commented, "I seem to be asking an awful lot of questions". The man replied, "It's better that way. My head is so confused I don't know what to talk about. There is so much, and as if [sic] there is nothing". When I was able to use my countertransference I could find an empathic comment like, "It's very hard to have to deal with so many uncertainties", and he could reply, "Yes, you're right. What can you do?"

Whereas in private practice I would rely on the patient being able to free-associate in some way, even to confusion, here it was much harder. It was difficult to leave silences in case we lost each other. In some way, not having a shared language appeared to create anxiety that we would not be able to maintain shared thinking across silence. Also I felt, perhaps mistakenly, that my interpreter would find silences difficult to understand.

I have been forced to reconsider many issues of technique in this work and to consider where it requires an adaptation of traditional psychoanalytic technique. There is always the possibility that my adaptation may be defensive, in which case I would need to find some other way of meeting the difficulty.

Comment from neuroscience

Freud's work and writing as founder of psychoanalysis grew out of his first training as a neurologist, and he always believed that one day discoveries about the mind and the brain would be able to come together. From the mid-twentieth century onwards, this has been increasingly the case, and neuroscientists are bringing particular insights to work with trauma. I shall quote as an example Jaak Panksepp, recognized as an authority on the basic brain circuitry shared by all mammals. In *Affective Neuroscience* (1998) he describes the basic emotional circuitry whereby sensory stimuli influence motor response and sustain arousal after the precipitating events have passed. These systems interact with cognitive input to produce adaptive response, and are particularly important to the animal's survival needs. "Emotional circuits have reciprocal interactions with the brain mechanisms that elaborate higher decision-making processes and consciousness" (Panksepp, 1998, p. 49).

> To be overwhelmed by an emotional experience means that the intensity is such that other brain mechanisms such as higher rational processes are disrupted because of the spontaneous behavioral and affective dictates of the more primitive brain control systems. [1998, p. 47]

Here I am concerned with the differences involved in work with refugees, where their internal disturbance is the result of massive external traumatic input, threatening physical survival. In these circumstances primitive levels of brain function come into play, needed in primitive situations of physical need for survival by all mammals.

Jaak Panksepp proposes four basic emotional circuits, common to all mammals: seeking, fear, panic and rage, each of which supports related behaviour, and interacts and connects with higher level systems. In normal circumstances, inter-connectivity between these basic systems and higher level organization is maintained, as well as continuing search for more information from the external world. The interconnectivity, however, and search for input from external stimuli, are interrupted when fear is too great, and thereby the ability to process information is cut short.

In my observation of work with some refugee clients I think that all their basic systems would have been stimulated to an unmanageable level, leading to a loss of normal self-regulatory confidence. Three years after their flight from external threat they still experience an underlying state of mental confusion with a primitive quality, as if experience cannot be sorted out.

The need is for therapy to provide some reflective opportunity within a secure framework of time and space to allow normal processes to resume.

Dissociation

In my short experience of a different kind of therapy with refugee clients, I have observed in them states of confusion and helplessness. As Freud says, the mind responds to threat of trauma "with every possible defence". In such circumstances the most typical defence would seem to be some kind of dissociation.

In *Fetishism* (1927), Freud describes a form of dissociation whereby the ego splits itself in order to be able to hold at the same time two beliefs which are incompatible. This would be designed to avoid pain, grief or anxiety at facing a truth. He gives the example of two young men who had each lost a father in boyhood. They had avoided reality by managing to both know and disavow their father's death.

It was only one current in their mental life that had not recognised their father's death; there was another current which took full account of that fact. The attitude which fitted in with the wish and the attitude which fitted in with reality existed side by side. [Freud, 1927, pp. 156]

This type of dissociation to avoid a truth which feels unbearable also prevents the ego from coming to terms with some part of reality. In the work I have been describing, facts of the more recent past often seem hazy. I feel hesitant to pursue major questions with the clients: for example, whether their parents are alive or dead. It appears as if the reality is either unknowable or unbearable. Sometimes the woman will talk about her mother as if she is present in her life; sometimes any questions meet a blank response. It may be that, as in Freud's example, my clients are holding beliefs both that their parents are alive, and that they are dead. Certainly there is little evident attempt to find out what the reality might be.

A different and opposite problem exists for them in dealing with the future. In reality, in the near future two contrary possibilities exist, namely that they may, or may not, be allowed to stay here. In this case, the terrible pain of uncertainty about the future is dealt with by holding on to one or other possibility as a reality. Either there is a conviction that they will have to go, or a bland optimism that they will be able to stay. It has been hard for me as a therapist to help my clients hold together the reality of two future possibilities, and an unknown outcome.

A variation of technique

The dread of being "removed" or "returned" is always present just below the surface, but rarely spoken about. Instead there is often a strange shallow reality which has neither the depth of the past nor projection into the future. When the clients' removal seemed very likely, I felt that I had to approach it with them in some way. Taking this to supervision, I was advised, "Help them think practically. If they have to go, what would they need to take?" (Thomas, 2003). This approach enabled us to touch the feelings involved, as it were incidentally. This illustrates a particular quality of the work. Where external reality has been so destructive and disrupting, internal states can sometimes be approached by focusing on external issues. This may facilitate containment. Anything which supports these clients' capability and confidence to manage in practical terms, whatever the external situation they have to face, can be therapeutic. Some clients' internal states are so terrifying that they have to be mediated by the holding of external practical reality.

This is an important difference of technique. In the tradition of psychoanalytic psychotherapy we are likely to focus on an under-standing of internal states and unconscious phantasy, closely related to work in the transference. (The particular quality of transference in the work with refugees will be taken up again later.)

Somatization

Attempts to make links between past, present and future, or between the external and internal reality, often founder. Dissociated pain, fear and anger take on somatic forms which move around the body and defy medical diagnosis. The bodily pain carries dissoci-ated psychic pain which it has been impossible to process in the mind. This is not unfamiliar with patients in traditional practice. The somatic communication, however, is a very frequent form of expres-sion for refugee clients. The body speaks directly; it is our earliest experience of ourselves before language. Regression to the somatic seems particularly likely in situations where primitive fears of non-survival have been aroused.

In traditional psychotherapy we may interpret the symptom, or attempt to place it in some meaningful context of experience. In working with clients from a different cultural background and trad-ition, it often seems as if interpretation has little to offer. Concepts of unconscious communication, which are now widely accepted in the society we belong to, may be far outside the conceptual world of our clients in the Refugee Therapy Centre. It is hard to pick up the message from bodily pain in a way which conveys appreciation of both physical and psychical reality.

This again sounds like "what every therapist knows": but the task of addressing somatic symptoms in therapy with clients from a different cultural tradition means that the therapist has to be aware of many different assumptions about the body–mind relationship within the clients' culture.

Impact of trauma on the ability to symbolize

The need to survive narrows the horizon of the mind. Where there is fear of annihilation, the mind focuses on whatever concrete reality seems most immediately relevant. Thus trauma destroys the ability to symbolize, and make connections of meaning. Jaak Panksepp writes that trauma interrupts the wider interconnectivity of brain systems, and prevents the primitive basic circuits searching for new information. Trauma interrupts the ability to put experience into language, and to link it to other mental content.

Over time, the wife of the couple with whom I have been working recovered a good deal of vitality in her daytime life, but continued to complain of very bad nights. She would wake up in states of terror, but could describe no images or specific fears. For a long time she could report nothing like a dream, only a vague sense of threatening darkness or evil presence. We returned to the night-time fears many times, and eventually she brought some bizarre and horrifying dream fragments. This seemed to me an exciting indication of progress; but, strangely, neither she nor I could associate to, or elaborate on, the fragments in any way. They appeared dissociated from symbolic meaning, and no connections could be made. When we paid close attention to any dream fragments that she could bring, gradually they became less bizarre and some narrative began to appear. With her, however, my ability to associate seemed disrupted, compared to my usual experience in working with dreams.

Jose Saporta, who is both a psychoanalyst and a neuroscientist, addresses the theme of the impact of trauma upon the ability to symbolize. He writes:

> Memories (i.e. conscious, verbal or "episodic" memory) are formed only when experience can be encoded and organized symbolically. With severe trauma there is a failure to encode and organize the experience at a symbolic level . . . there is a continuum in the degree to which, and coherence with which, experiences are represented and organized symbolically . . . there are no words or linguistic categories to contain, organize or articulate trauma. Without words or symbols there is no meaning and no imaginative elaboration. [Saporta, 2003, pp. 98–9]

Saporta continues:

There are different levels, then, at which information can be excluded from integrated conscious awareness. On one level information has not been encoded in symbolic form and remains in subsymbolic form. This is often the mechanism for the inability to represent trauma ... At another level, information that has been encoded as verbal symbols may be blocked due to conflict or painful affect, or its meaning disavowed. [p. 103]

He describes "the concrete and blunt immediacy of traumatic experience which obliterates perspective ... Language holds out hope for restoring subjectivity and meaning following their collapse in the face of trauma" (p. 102).

In attempting to enter into the dreams or daytime experiences of clients who have suffered traumatic impairment of their mental functioning I experience my own functioning to be impaired. It is often only after a session that I can think about a somatic symptom or associate to a dream fragment with any conviction. Saporta writes about the damage to the sense of self where self-regulation, symbolization and subjectivity have been impaired by trauma. In my experience the therapist's capability to think and symbolize may also be affected, and may have to be regained outside of the session. I would see this phenomenon as a form of dissociation, where meaning and language are disconnected through trauma.

Impact of trauma on memory

Current research by cognitive psychologists amplifies our understanding of memory systems. Brewin (2003) describes the existence of two memory systems: one more primitive and activated under extreme fear, one more complex and allowing greater subtlety of processing:

A key part of the brain is the amygdala, a small area in the temporal lobe adjacent to the hippocampus. The amygdala is responsible for initiating a variety of biologically hard-wired responses to threat, including release of stress hormones, activation of the sympathetic nervous system, and behaviors such as fighting, fleeing and freezing. Information about threat is conveyed from the sense organs to the amygdala via a number of separate pathways. [Brewin, 2003, p. 116]

He tells us that there are more primitive direct routes which activate defence responses very quickly but at a simplified perceptual level. "These subcortical pathways mainly process information at the level of individual perceptual features such as color, shape or direction of movement" (p. 117). By contrast there are alternative routes involving more brain areas including the hippocampus and some cortical structures, "all of which project independently to the amygdala". All of these pathways allow more complex and integrative processing in the context of space and time. "In evolutionary terms these parts of the brain are more recent. The pathways involve more synapses and are slower but they permit a much more complex analysis of what is in the environment that is most closely associated with the fearful event" (p. 117).

In the work with the couple which I have been describing, I have seen their great difficulty in accessing any coherent memory of trauma. Apart from natural resistance to revisiting intense fear and panic, it appears that stretches of narrative are missing. Whether, in Saporta's terms, these memory links were never encoded, or whether they were encoded and then blanked out, it is hard to tell. The couple could only access isolated sensory details, particularly of sight and touch. They could say, "When everyone fled from the village one night it was very dark . . . we held hands not to lose each other . . . in the forest we couldn't see each other until the moon came out". These intense moments burned in through the senses stand out indelibly.

Many of the symptoms affecting refugees would match the description of post traumatic stress disorder (PTSD) given in *DSM IV*, 1994, where an objective description is given of stressors and responses. Witnessing actual or threatened death or serious injury is a typical stressor; helplessness, trauma in flashback, avoidance, confusion of past and present are typical responses. Brewin links current research with the work of Janet in *L'amnesie et la dissociation de souvenir par l'emotion* (1904).

> Janet proposed that extremely frightening experiences might be unable to be assimilated into a person's ordinary beliefs, assumptions and meaning structures; in which case they would be stored in a different form, "dissociated" from conscious awareness and involuntary control. Traumatic memory was inflexible and fixed, in

contrast to narrative memory which was adaptable to current circumstances. [Brewin, 2003, p. 108]

Very possibly in private practice we meet patients suffering PTSD as a result, for example, of accident or bereavement. We work with them to process and link the experience with all the mental resources which may have been disrupted. In work with refugees, however, there is a difference in scale. The impact of the external threat is not just upon an individual but upon a whole community or ethnic group. Terror may have lasted for years; a whole environment may have been devastated. Their experience may leave the therapist feeling helpless and disorientated, unable to be in any way effective.

Renos Papadopoulos cautions against generalizing or patholo-gizing refugees. He writes:

> Although refugees do not constitute any one coherent diagnostic category of psychological or psychopathological characteristics, the fact that they have all lost their homes makes them share a deep sense of nostalgic yearning for restoring that very specific type of loss. [Papadopoulos, 2002, p. 15]

He elaborates the various meanings of "home" in terms of origin and future, physical and imaginary, external and internal, and speaks of the "mosaic substratum of identity".

> It is important to appreciate that disturbance of the mosaic sub-stratum creates a kind of loss that could be characterized as primary, as opposed to all the secondary losses which are of a tangible nature and of which the person is aware. [*ibid.*, p. 18]

This description enables me better to orientate myself in my work with refugees. The Refugee Therapy Centre is a place that approaches being some kind of a home and point of reorientation for people suffering "nostalgic disorientation – this uniqueness of the refugee predicament" (Papadopoulos, 2002, p. 15). I have learned that in my clients' culture, "relationship" in terms of the community is the key to personal identity. Each member of the village is recognized as part of an extended family. To lose contact with this cultural matrix disrupts the whole security of personal identity. Importantly, each person was needed and able to contribute to the communal life, at home. This work challenges me to think about a different kind of transference related to a fear of social annihilation. The meaning of relationship within the therapy has to be seen in a social context.

Transference and survival

Thinking about the transference in this context is complicated when the need for survival in the external world has been an urgent concern and preoccupation. The therapist is first of all representative of the host society. To begin with the clients are probably careful not to complain. They fear rejection, and recognize dependence for life-support through benefits, since they are not allowed to work. The therapist has the huge advantage of belonging in this society, holding a passport, privileged in every way. There is ambivalence, inevitably. The therapist is "someone who knows how things are done here", and should be able to help. Such a situation can raise feelings of humiliation at the inequality, and envy of the therapist's secure belonging.

Being a representative of the host society is an especially powerful issue around any times of immigration hearing. The therapist is likely to feel particularly identified with the client's wish to be accepted and offered status: and the client is likely to experience the therapist as an ally. On the other hand the therapist is powerless to affect the external decision, and is part of the potentially rejecting society. It has been hard, but also necessary, to address such situations if the therapy were not to stagnate. When I have struggled to put this ambiguity into words, my comments have been received and the atmosphere lifted.

The transference is powerfully cultural as well as personal and it is necessary to keep both in mind. One outcome of the therapy I am describing is that both clients are now able at times to express anger and grievance at experiences here. It has been important for the therapist to be able to receive these negative projections and hold them.

The transference is also to the Refugee Therapy Centre as a substitute for "home". As Renos Papadopoulos described, nostalgia for home is the experience all refugees share. For the clients, the building is an environment designed to welcome them, and it fulfils this purpose very well. Much thought has been given to creating rooms where clients can have some sense of being at home. There are harmonious colours and comfortable furnishings, and lots of toys for children. Above all, there are many pictures of people from all over the world, giving clients a chance to find some identification in the space. It is an environment full of vitality and interest. For the refugee clients, it provides continuity, support for their identity and a place where they are known. It has become a community with its own structures and relationships, where refugees and members of a host society belong together.

Transference to the therapist is many layered; the therapist is representative of the host society and also of the Refugee Therapy Centre, and also carrier of more personal projections. I have been aware of the woman's powerful need of a maternal figure, and her isolation from feminine support. During the first year of therapy, when she was beginning to speak more freely, she brought photos and documents relating to the baby they had lost. The sense that the couple needed a person to witness personal loss was powerful and immediate. The wife also needed maternal support during the third pregnancy. In this situation, as in more traditional settings, the therapist has to survive in order to be available. To survive effectively requires finding a difficult balance between the external and internal world. The pull towards the clients' tangible needs is strong. I have often felt envy of those with legal or medical expertise. It is not uncommon for therapists to fantasize about offering refugees a home or financial support. It is a constant effort to translate experience into words that can link up different levels of experience and meaning. It also depends greatly on the skill of the interpreter, which could be the subject of a chapter in itself. Transference to the interpreter can be much simpler than to the therapist. There is direct contact through language. In my case the interpreter was of a similar age to the clients and they had shared similar experiences. I detected no ambivalence in their relationship to her.

The link between myself and the interpreter has been crucial. Together we are part of a holding professional environment. We talk briefly together before and after every session. We have different roles, but share the experience of bearing witness to the clients' lives. At times when fears of non-survival recede, we think with our clients about future plans. Whether they have to leave, or whether they can stay, there are avenues and possibilities to explore.

Acknowledgements

My particular thanks are due to Aida Alayarian, Clinical Director of the Refugee Therapy Centre, for her inspiring leadership, help and support; to Josephine Klein for her valuable comments on this chapter, and her encouragement; to Anisa Nura, my interpreter, who is a fine partner who has contributed greatly to the work; and to Lennox Thomas for his enabling supervision and wealth of cultural insight. The work described took place at The Refugee Therapy Centre, now at 40 St. Johns Way, London N19 3RR.

CHAPTER THREE

Racism as a borderline issue: the avoidance and marginalization of race in psychotherapy

Frank Lowe

"Nations and peoples are largely the stories they feed themselves. If they tell themselves stories that are lies, they will suffer the future consequences of those lies. If they tell themselves stories that face their own truths, they will free their histories for future flowerings."

Ben Okri, *Birds of Heaven* (1996)

This chapter highlights the failure of psychoanalysis to face its own truths about issues of race and white racism in the selection and training of psychotherapists and in the delivery of psychotherapy. It explores possible reasons for this failure and calls for action to make psychotherapy less racially exclusive and more responsive to the needs of a multiracial and multicultural society.

Much has been written about psychotherapy as a predominantly white middle-class activity. In Britain this concern has led to the development of intercultural therapy as a way of addressing psychotherapy's inaccessibility to people from black and ethnic minority communities. The work of Jaffar Kareem, Lennox Thomas and Fahad Dalal has stimulated numerous seminars and conferences on psychotherapy, race and culture. However, despite increased

43

awareness, the evidence suggests that these issues are generally avoided or marginalized by the profession.

In 1993, a survey by the Runnymede Trust found that only 5 out of 33 psychoanalytic training organizations had a formal written equal opportunities policy. The conclusion drawn from this survey was that although a handful of organizations had made considerable progress, psychotherapy-training organizations in the main had yet to address equal opportunities in any serious way (Gordon, 1993). Has much progress been made since and how is it evidenced? It is an area that will benefit from more research, but the available evidence suggests that not much has changed and there are no grounds for complacency or defensiveness. The McPherson Report in 1999 recommended that all organizations, not just the police, should examine their policies and the outcome of their policies and practices, to guard against disadvantaging any section of the community. A few psychotherapeutic institutions such as the Tavistock Clinic, responded to this call and began a process of critical review. However, the days of inaction may be numbered as a result of recent legislative developments, primarily the Human Rights Act 1998 and the Race Relations Amendment Act 2000. The latter outlaws race discrimination and places a duty to promote race equality not just on the public sector but also on private bodies with public functions. Therefore psychotherapy organizations should for legal, if not for moral reasons, examine the implications of these Acts for their operations and consider their position as regards matters of diversity and race equality.

Racism is an emotive and highly complex issue. It has economic roots, is both psychological and ideological, and operates at individual, organizational and social levels. It can broadly be described either

> as division of humankind into fixed, closed and unalterable groups or as a systematic domination of some groups by others . . . It may be based on colour or physical features or culture, nationality and way of life; it may affirm equality of human worth but implicitly deny this by insisting on the superiority of a particular culture; it may admit equality up to a point but impose a glass ceiling higher up. Whatever its subtle disguises and forms, it is deeply divisive, intolerant of differences, a source of much human suffering, and inimical to a common sense of belonging [Runnymede Trust, 2000, p. ix]

There is a tendency to think about racism as a universal or even natural phenomenon, but this is unhelpful because it is inaccurate and obscures the reality of individual and social experience. There have been many significantly different racisms – each historically specific and articulated in a different way in the societies in which they appear, whatever the common features they may share (Gilroy *et al.*, 1982). This paper is concerned with white racism, which is rooted in a specific period of British and European socio-economic history.

Institutional racism

Before the explorations of Columbus in the fifteenth century, black people, as Christians, were able to rise to prominence within European society. With the advent of colonization and slavery, racist ideas emerged about black inferiority and the existence of races and a racial hierarchy. By the nineteenth and early twentieth century Charles Darwin's ideas were used to give pseudo-scientific credibility to racism, and acceptance of the existence of a racial hierarchy and white superiority was widespread. Although we no longer live in a world of colonies and eugenics societies, the power relationship between Europe and its former colonies, between whites and blacks, is still not equal. Race continues to be a category of social and psychological stratification, and through this the myth of biological races, of white superiority and black inferiority, continues, albeit in a different shape and form.

Until the Stephen Lawrence Inquiry, "middle England" liked to believe that only an extremist minority was responsible for racism in society. This "rotten apples" perspective was discredited by the McPherson report which acknowledged the existence of institutionalized racism in British society. McPherson defined institutional racism as

> the collective failure of an organisation to provide an appropriate and professional service to people because of their colour, culture or ethnic origin. It can be detected in processes, attitudes and behaviours which amount to discrimination through unwitting prejudice, ignorance, thoughtlessness and racist stereotyping which disadvantages ethnic minority people. [Macpherson, 1999]

For example, the over-representation of African-Caribbeans in mental health services has been noted for at least two decades, as has the finding that black and ethnic minority mental health patients are more likely to receive high levels of medication, and less likely to receive non-physical treatment such as psychotherapy and counselling (Littlewood and Lipsedge, 1982; Mental Health Foundation 1999; NIMHE, 2003). Despite the mass of research findings of racial discrimination and disadvantage in Britain, many white Britons find it hard to give up their fantasy of Britain as a fair and tolerant society and to accept the reality of racism, personal and institutional, in its various guises and forms.

Psychoanalytic psychotherapy, like other institutions in Britain, is not immune from racism, and an open non-defensive review of its approach to race equality is long overdue. This is necessary if the profession is to ensure that black and ethnic minority people are not excluded from its ranks or disadvantaged by its services.

Racism in psychoanalytic theory

In early twentieth-century psychology and psychoanalysis a model of the psyche was developed that reflected the belief in the existence of a racial hierarchy and white superiority. Black people were called savage or primitive and were represented as steeped in emotion, having a weak ego, possessing no will or self- control, prone to projection and not in full control of their thinking. The black adult was portrayed as functioning at the same level as the white child and within the psyche the black conscious was equated with the white unconscious. Stanley Hall (1904) in the well-known textbook on adolescence, described Asians, Chinese, Africans and indigenous Americans as "adolescent races". He believed that certain primitive races, like children, are in a state of immature development and must be treated gently and understandingly by more developed peoples. Freud (1913) in *Totem and Taboo* saw similarities between the "psychology of primitive peoples and the psychology of neurotics" and to him primitive peoples were savages or half savages and included Polynesians, Malayans, the native people of Australia, North and South America and the black races of Africa. He argued,

There are men still living who, as we believe stand very near to primitive man, far nearer than we do, and whom we therefore regard as his direct heirs and representatives. Such is our view of those whom we describe as savages or half-savages, and their mental life must have a peculiar interest for us if we are right in seeing in it a well-preserved picture of an early stage of our own development. [Freud, 1913, p. 53]

He also shared and reinforced the popular view of black people as sexually unrestrained beings: "We should certainly not expect the sexual life of these poor naked cannibals would be moral in our sense or that their sexual instincts would be subjected to any great degree of restriction" (Freud, 1913, p. 54)

Jung, the other great father of analytic psychotherapy, is even blunter.

These people live from their affects, are moved and have their being in emotion. Their consciousness takes care of their orientation in space and transmits impressions from the outside, and it is also stirred by inner impulses and affects. But is not given to reflection; the ego has almost no autonomy. The situation is not so different from the European; but we are after all somewhat more complicated. At any rate the European posses a certain measure of will and directed intention. [Jung, 1963, p. 270]

Jung is commonly taught and presented as a great humanist thinker. His concept of the collective unconscious suggests that he believes in a common humanity, but in fact it contains a racial hierarchy (Dalal, 1988). Addressing whites, Jung wrote that

In the collective unconscious you are the same as a man of another race, you have the same archetypes, just as you have, like him, eyes, a heart, a liver, and so on. It does not matter that his skin is black. It matters to a certain extent, sure enough – he probably has a whole historic layer less than you. [Jung, 1939a Vol. 18, p. 46]

Jung also had views on multiracial society, which is not too dissimilar from views expressed today about the effects of immigration on British Anglo-Saxon society. At the Second Psychoanalytic Congress (1910) he argued "Living together with the barbarous races, has a suggestive effect on the laboriously subjugated instincts of the white race and drags it down". He later wrote

> What is more contagious than to live side by side with a rather primitive people? . . . you call it going black . . . It is much easier for us Europeans to be a trifle immoral, or at least a bit, because we do not have to maintain the moral standard against the heavy downward pull of primitive life. The inferior man has a tremendous pull because he fascinates the inferior layers of our psyche, which has lived through untold ages of similar conditions . . . He reminds us not so much of our conscious as our unconscious mind – not only of childhood but also of prehistory. [Jung, 1939b, Vol. 10, p. 507]

It is significant that the profession does not discuss or teach about racism in its early history. Farhad Dalal's (1988) exposé of Jung's racism illustrates well the profession's selective blindness to racism. This paper contends that the selective blindness to racism in its past is not unrelated to its current blindness and inaction today. Unsurprisingly, it has fallen predominantly though not exclusively to black therapists who by virtue of their cultural backgrounds and experience cannot be blind to this history or silent about race in psychotherapy today.

Psychodynamics of racism

Although the contemporary psychoanalytic psychotherapy profession does not tackle racism as a serious problem, there have been a number of psychoanalytic papers on racism and there is a growing body of literature on the subject, e.g. Rustin (1991), Young (1994), Timimi (1996), Morgan (1998), Gordon (1993) and Garner (2003). Psychoanalytic thinking has undoubtedly made significant contributions to our understanding of the dynamics of racism. In general racism is seen as deeply configured in the psyche and racist dynamics are recognised as primitive and infantile in character. Thomas (1992) argued that to work across cultures and with people of different colour, psychotherapists need first to attend to their own racism, their own prejudices and projections onto other racial and cultural groups. A number of therapists such as Davids (1988) and Morgan (1998) have identified fear and blindness to uncomfortable aspects of ourselves, particularly as regards racial difference. Tan (1993) shows how similarity can be used as a defence against the painful feelings of difference. He for example defined racism as "an inability to accept and acknowledge difference without attempting to control and dominate the object that is felt to be different and separate" (1993, p. 42). Racism is thought of here as an organized defence system, residing in the primitive part of the self that is split off from awareness. The deployment of primitive defences (denial, splitting, projection, projective identification), to not own or face feelings about racial and cultural difference, is undoubtedly a major theme running through the literature, which in my view operates at both the individual and organizational level. This is described as "turn-ing a blind eye" (Davids, 1988), "loud silence" (Young, 1994), "keep-ing therapy white" (Gordon, 1993), and goes back to Freud, the father himself, who was also silent, at least publicly, about racism despite his experience of racial persecution as a Jew.

Understanding the psychic motives, mechanisms and processes involved in racism is helpful for those concerned with working with individuals and groups. However, more work needs to be done to understand psychoanalytically the management of race issues in analytic organizations. This work is largely avoided or treated not as a general and pervasive necessity but as a minority political issue. This is largely because psychoanalysis and psychoanalytic training organizations are white dominated institutions both in terms of their membership and culture and as this work isn't given much attention they are likely to remain so. But psychoanalysis is not just white; it also occupies a privileged social and economic position, and as is known from history, individuals as well as groups tend to protect their socio-economic interests, consciously and unconsciously, and do not give up power and privilege without struggle.

Institutional racism cannot be addressed by providing slots for race issues, or niches for black staff. There must be a systematic review of analytic organizations' ways of functioning, in terms of whether and how they disadvantage black and minority com-munities. This would include the selection of psychotherapists for training, content of training programmes and supervision arrange-ments. Overall this is about changing organizational culture and developing a non-defensive but non-persecutory approach to exploring racism rather than avoidance, denial and splitting it off from awareness at the intra-psychic, interpersonal, group and organizational levels. Although facing the subject, through more open dialogue and thought, is likely to be painful, it is also more likely to lead to action that will help the profession become more inclusive and culturally diverse. This will involve confronting race myths and stereotypes about the self and the racial other, breaking down racial divides and boundaries and developing a profession that is less prone to self-idealization and more broad based in its representations and concerns. For if anti-racism is about anything, it is about whole-object relating, which means really recognizing that the world is not black and white, and that the self is not all good and the other is not all bad. For whites it is about taking responsibility for the construction of the primitive, the savage, inferior black other either unconsciously or consciously. This of course means working in the depressive position.

Race and racism are clinical issues

There is a tendency in analytic institutions to see race and racism as political issues. Nevertheless there is a small but growing body of psychoanalytic literature on cultural and racial difference and the challenges it throws up in the consulting room (Evans Holmes, 1992, Timimi, 1996, Garner, 2003). I provide below two brief examples which I hope will help illustrate this.

Example 1

A black professional woman made many enquiries to find herself a black male therapist. After many months of trying she eventually found me. At our initial meeting she started by saying how pleased she was to have found me. She then talked easily and with relief about her history. I heard a tale of survival and success against great odds and immense childhood trauma. She had grown up witnessing a high level of domestic violence in the Caribbean, where she spent the first ten years of her life. Her father had a violent temper and would beat his children if they made him cross. Towards the end of the session, as we were agreeing the terms of the work, she began questioning me about my training. She wanted to know where I had trained, and what was my orientation. She expressed surprise that patients used a couch, as she thought that the couch was a relic of the nineteenth century and was really passé, a bit like Freud. This felt like an attack and in the counter-transference I felt I was being pushed to say that I was able and trustworthy. I thought she was expressing anxiety about starting therapy and was worried in particular about whether I was a safe therapist, and wouldn't attack her as her father had done. Although this patient was able to make some use of this largely conventional interpretation it proved of limited value. She was not just concerned about whether I would be a violent father; she also wanted to know what kind of black man I was. Was I real or was I really white on the inside with my Freudian training? Could I be trusted?

For this patient, exploring the black father was important and it was important that her therapist understood that. But my largely colour-blind training had not adequately prepared me for this encounter. The patient did not return and there may have been many reasons for this. However, I felt that my failure to recognize the importance race had for her was at least one of them.

This vignette also contains a common difficulty for many therapists, i.e. if they can see race is an issue for a patient, whether, how and when they should address this, especially when patient and therapist are still strangers to each other and are still in the process of negotiating a contract. My experience suggests that if race is clearly an issue, it should be named as this conveys to the patient that the therapist has the capacity or at least the willingness to work with this issue, and the patient's anxieties about it. This is more likely to give relief and be containing for the patient. Avoidance on the other hand is likely to suggest that neither the patient or therapist can be trusted to handle the subject.

Example 2

Tunde was 15. He was born in South London, the only son of an African mother. He was referred for therapy because of concerns by his school that he was being bullied regularly and consequently was increasingly withdrawing from school. He had been the victim of bullying since age 11, but more recently he was being bullied by black boys about his racial identity, i.e. he was told he was not black. His "friends" were Asian boys but Tunde was really contemptuous of them, and wasn't close to anyone.

In his assessment by a white therapist, he offered a brief history. He was brought up by his mother but had two episodes of brief contact with his father. The first was at around age 4 for a short period when he vaguely remembers meeting his father, but he disappeared, to re-emerge when he was around age 9. According to Tunde, his father's contact appeared more motivated by his wanting a relationship with his mother than by him having any real interest in him. After a short period his father disappeared again and Tunde hasn't seen him since. His mother was a counselling student and recognized the value of therapy and had insisted that he saw a therapist. Tunde described his school as not academic and dominated by a gangster culture, with pupils mugging other pupils and teachers, who he thought were frightened of pupils.

At his first consultation appointment, he talked about not enjoying any aspect of school life. He didn't refer to being bullied but was very critical of other pupils, who he thought were on their way to being gangsters. He described the teachers as either weak or absent. Tunde often felt prejudged by others and thought he was probably seen by whites on the street as a mugger and nothing else. The therapist thought he seemed very alienated from those around him and was struggling to fit into the world as a young black man. Tunde was late for both of his consultation appointments and the therapist interpreted this as his finding it difficult to talk about his difficulties and that he was probably very embarrassed about them.

As a result of a suggestion by a member of the clinical team, the case was referred to me because she had thought that a black male therapist might be useful to Tunde. At our first meeting, Tunde communicated a strong unease if not unhappiness about being in my consulting room. I shared my impression with him. He said that I was correct, because he had only come because his mother had insisted. I asked why his mother thought it was important that he came against his will. He explained that she genuinely cared about him and was worried about the effects of problems he had had at school with other pupils as well as teachers. But he was fine now because he was not attending school. I asked about his experience of the consultation and the recommendation that he could benefit from therapy. Tunde shrugged and said he hadn't taken it seriously because he felt that the therapist had been like a supply teacher. I asked him to elaborate. But he simply repeated, "you know, like a supply teacher". I commented that he might be letting me know that he was unsure about whether to take me seriously and to make a commitment to the therapy, because I might also be like a supply teacher, like the other therapist. Tunde didn't comment.

In the context of exploring his relationships, I asked about his father. He smiled and said "everybody thinks my father is important but he isn't and he doesn't mean a thing to me. I hardly know the man and because he was never around, I do not miss him." I said that he sounded as if he did not value his dad at all, and had pushed him aside as he might have felt pushed aside and not valued by him. Tunde said that he had a wider family and had a good grandmother with whom he got on. I said that he might be wondering about what kind of black man I was; would I be like his father or someone with whom he gets along? After a brief silence, Tunde became animated and spoke about how damaged black people were. That they were at the bottom of the food chain, poorest and without economic, political or social power. He spoke of black boys at school talking big but doing little. Obsessed with fashionable clothes and music and only being interested in sex. He felt black people really hate themselves as for example lots of black female pop stars, such as Jamelia, wore wigs for aesthetic not practical reasons. I was surprised by his change of energy and acutely observed analysis of black people that he communicated and asked him to say why he thought that these things were a manifestation of self-hate. Tunde then informed me that he had been attending an awareness group for black children, which was alright, and that they were learning lots about black history.

After a slow start, with frequent lateness, and missed sessions, Tunde has gradually increased his attendance at therapy and is showing a willingness to explore his relationship with his mother, and to face his need for, but fear and anger with, his father as he seeks to establish an adult black male identity.

Discussion

Although Tunde did not state that his race/culture/identity was a problem at the point of referral, it was clear that race was part of the presenting problem, i.e. he was being bullied by other black boys for not being black. Yet this issue was not named or explored in his assessment. I think it is significant that the white therapist assessing Tunde did not think it appropriate to consider whether Tunde's engagement/lack of engagement might be related to race issues whether in the therapist or patient.

Tunde clearly was relieved and I believe encouraged to hear that I was able to speak about these issues – which I think were deeply troubling for him. In the transference I feel that I am both important and close to Tunde – but I equally feel as a wary object, one that he isn't sure about and needs to work out. This is a long haul not just about race issues (blackness, whiteness and in particular black masculinity) but also about an enmeshed relationship between mother and son and difficulties about separation. The fear of race, race-blindness and being blinded by race are all dangers in this case.

Evans Holmes (1992) observed that patients and therapists often collude both in same-race and in cross-race therapy by focusing more on external factors to explain patient's multi-faceted conflicts. A black patient seeing a white therapist may feel like a traitor, or may see the whiteness of the therapist as an idealized lost object. Or a white patient or black patient seeing a black therapist may feel doubtful about the therapist's authority, be rivalrous or expect magical understanding from "someone who knows what it is like to be a victim". White therapist guilt, black therapist over-identification, and fear of conflict and aggression in therapists and patients are some of the factors that can limit therapeutic work in this area.

The idea that the patient and the therapist may have active ideas about each other, based on ethnicity, before the pair meet has been developed by Kareem (1992) as "societal transference" and Thomas (1992) as the "pre-transference". Kareem argued that it was the responsibility of the therapist to bring these issues into the open in the therapeutic encounter, as the client/patient may be too anxious or vulnerable to have taken responsibility for this inevitably difficult process. But the lack of attention to race issues in their training leaves many therapists unprepared and unsure about how to work with race in the consulting room. As a result many patients and therapists keep away from the unsettling and scary feelings which race arouses.

Morgan (1998), a white therapist, has usefully elucidated how colour-blindness can be used as a mechanism of denial and defence against fear. Growing recognition that intolerance of difference is characteristic of paranoid-schizoid thinking has increased our understanding of the importance of exploring unconscious dynamics in the transference and countertransference within black/white professional relationships. Lennox Thomas has written about the need for the dynamics of intercultural therapy to be an essential part of psychotherapy training. This chapter adds to this call but argues more specifically that it is the dynamic of racism, which is more frightening and challenging and difficult to think about, that is avoided and consequently remains unnoticed in the consulting room and leads to limited, unconfident and at times defensive therapeutic practice.

In my view Evans Holmes (1992) has correctly argued that race is not the only factor whose full utilization in analysis has been limited by countertransference problems and conceptual myths and that it can in fact be a potentially useful facilitator of transference reactions. She reported clinical examples of how her "race" was used by patients to organize and project their feelings of inferiority.

> The fact of racial difference is probably as powerful a trigger and container for the projection of unacceptable impulses – with resulting prejudices toward the object of projection – as we have in our culture. Thus it is not likely that in the therapeutic situation transference and counter-transference strains related to race can ever be reduced to zero. [Evans Holmes, 1992, p. 2]

It would be a mistake to assume that race is relevant only in cross-race patient-therapist dyads. Reference to race in same-race dyads, be it black or white, do come up and should be thought about and interpreted. Fakhry Davids (1988) shows the value of therapy which helps the patient know about their hidden split-off part which permeates their relationships and limits their creativity. I believe that it was working in the transference with Tunde as the hated black (supply teacher) father which, though frightening and painful, engaged him and brought him alive in the therapy. It is therefore about facing transference issues including race and racism in the transference and valuing the analysis of the transference as opposed to avoidance that would help the patient. Being apologetic for or politely blind to transference issues, including race, can only be counter-therapeutic. Countertransference reactions related to race need proper consideration in supervision, in the therapist's own analysis and in training. It is time for the profession to respond to these issues through more case reports and discussion and in its approach to issues of race and racism in training.

Race and racism in training

I haven't met a black therapist or trainee therapist who has been satisfied with their training organization's handling of race issues or feels confident that the profession is addressing the problem. I have explored how colour blindness or race avoidance can occur as a defence against fear and helplessness and I believe it also operates at an institutional level as a mechanism to maintain power, i.e. the status quo with its traditional power relations, authority and control.

> Whenever I raise issues about race and culture, I am told this course is about the internal world not social issues. (Trainee child psychotherapist)

> I was asked about whether I would be able to work with white patients. I was surprised when I was not offered a place that one of the reasons given was that I had not spoken about race issues. But you don't know if you should or shouldn't talk about race. I thought not raising it was the most safe and sensible option. The interviewer assured me that my not getting in was nothing to do with my race because the Institute was a liberal place and would bend over backwards to have black trainees. I was angry and perplexed. (Black applicant to the Institute of Psychoanalysis)

> During my interview I was asked about working with white patients but none of my fellow white trainees were asked about their ability to work with black patients. (Black adult psychotherapist)

I feel isolated with my experience of the training and I do not feel confident that I will get support if I talk about my experience and views as a black person. I think it's probably best to just keep my head down and get through the training. (Black trainee adult psychotherapist)

These experiences raise a number of issues about psychoanalytic trainings, but they also tell a story about power and the lack of it. A power structure exists at present that is not ethnically diverse or committed to equality of opportunity and anti-discriminatory practice, a power structure that has not yet reflected on its racist history and its colonial legacy in a fast-changing multicultural, multiracial society. From a black perspective, there is an urgent need to review selection criteria and processes, and to consider what subjects and perspectives are relevant to a psychotherapy training today. What is needed is psychoanalytic psychotherapy training that want to attract trainees from all backgrounds, trainees who would feel enabled to think about their lives, experiences and cultures and be equipped to operate confidently as therapists with people from diverse racial and cultural backgrounds. If this is to be achieved, "thoughtlessness" about race and racism in psychoanalytic trainings cannot be allowed to continue.

A good enough training should enable trainees to achieve greater self-knowledge and be free of blind spots, or at least be aware of those which may interfere with their work. It should develop the capacity to think about emotional experiences and should discourage conformity and imitation or, in Winnicottian terms, the maintenance of a false self. It should also help therapists to cope better with depressive anxieties through a belief in their capacity and commitment to repair their internal and external objects and be creative. These outcomes will not be properly achieved when training organizations maintain a loud silence on race issues, for as Bernadi and Nieto (1992) have argued "we should talk more about what we do not yet know, or do not know well. This area of uncertainty is also the greatest potential for research and training" (p. 137).

The marginalization of racism – what can be done about it?

I have often been struck by the lack of capacity to talk about and think about race and racism in a profession which values talk and thinking, and sees itself as committed to truth however painful. This is indicative of a lack of reflection on this issue, which is institutionalized by its training arrangements. There is something quite bizarre about this, as is the experience of racism itself, and the way that it persists as a phenomenon in society despite advances in scientific knowledge about humans. There are I believe many similarities between the psychodynamics of racism and borderline phenomena:

1. Racism operates consciously, pre-consciously and unconsciously. Like the borderline case it can appear to be rational but in many ways is highly irrational and verges on insanity. I think it might be helpful to think of racism as borderline phenomena that lie on the frontier between neurosis and psychosis. Rycroft (1968) observed that the defence of borderline personalities is of a psychotic type, although the person's behaviour is not.

2. Racism arouses powerful feelings of helplessness, pain and rage, and a pressure to act out in the victim which requires immense containment. Our recognition of borderline personalities is based on the affective quality of the patient's communication and the analyst's own inner response to it – in particular the countertransference. Steiner (1987) writes that borderline patients have a tendency to massively project parts of the self and internal objects into the analyst, and to arouse in the analyst feelings of being helpless and at the mercy of vengeful exploitative behaviour whilst the patient remains impervious to the analyst's needs. How to bear these feelings and not become alienated and not think the patient is unanalysable is a major challenge for the analyst working with borderline cases. Racism involves similar processes and requires immense effort to contain powerful projections as well as manage highly stressful and painful feelings.

3. So keeping racism at the border, both consciously and unconsciously, could be seen as having a protective function, to prevent something becoming invaded/overwhelmed/

destroyed. A number of Kleinian writers (O' Shaughnessy, Bion, Steiner) have identified the operation of a defensive organization in borderline and other serious pathologies. This concept contains

> the idea of development of a structured pattern of impulses, anxieties and defences which root the personality somewhere between the paranoid and depressive positions. This pattern allows the individual to maintain a balance, a precarious but strongly defended one, in which he is protected from the chaos of the paranoid-schizoid position, that is, he does not become frankly psychotic, and yet he does not progress to a point where he can confront and try to work through the problems of the depressive position with their intrinsic pain. [Bott Spillius, 1988, pp. 195–196]

4. O' Shaunessy (1981) and Steiner (1987) see the defensive organization as a defence against both the fragmentation and confusion of the paranoid-schizoid position, but also of the mental pain and responsibilities of the depressive position which the ego finds impossible to negotiate. So efforts by the individual to make reparation, characteristic of the depressive position, are usually too narcissistic to bring about resolution. The defensive organization is seen as having a sort of pseudo integration, which can masquerade as the integration of the depressive position and give the illusion of providing relative stability and avoidance of depressive pain.

I believe that the borderline concept helps us think more clearly and realistically about the nature of racism, particularly its fort-like defensive system and its intransigence.

Thinking of white racism as borderline phenomena helps us better understand the white's inability to make contact with the black other because it arouses immense anxiety and there is a fear of loss, of fragmentation or dissolution of self and identity. Freud (1924) believed that neurosis does not disavow reality but only ignores it, whereas psychosis disavows it and tries to replace it. Freud is seeking here to elucidate that both neurosis and psychosis are a rebellion against the external world and this involves the loss of reality. Whilst in neurosis there is a flight from reality, in psychosis there is a stronger form of denial, even an active remodelling of reality. I believe the psychotherapy profession adopts both a neurotic (a flight from and ignoring of the reality of race and racism) and a psychotic response to race (a denial and remodelling of the reality of race and racism), in order to prevent a feared invasion from the outside or a shameful exposure of its insides. There is an unconscious fear of hidden racism being exposed and a conscious, sometimes stated fear that if the profession faces the realities of racism, it will lead to the profession becoming invaded by black political issues (anti-racism and equal opportunities) which in fantasy is construed as destructive crap. This or a slightly different variant is likely to be an organizational defensive rationale for not going there. There is fear that if racism is not kept at the margin/border, the consequences will be catastrophic.

Conclusion

The image of psychoanalytic psychotherapy as a white middle-class activity is still prevalent and must change. Although the number of black psychotherapists is increasing, black people are still very under-represented in the profession as well as amongst users of psychoanalytic psychotherapy. Although this chapter has focused on the avoidance of race and racism in psychoanalytic psychotherapy, it reflects a wider social struggle to achieve a less infantile approach to these issues. If psychoanalytic therapy is brave enough to face its borderline behaviour in relation to racism, I am confident that it will more positively engage with black and other alienated communities and not be seen as cut off from the reality that therapists, patients and training institutions are located in a society which is increasingly multicultural and diverse.

In this context the therapist's ability to accept and work with difference is increasingly critical. This ability is contingent upon the capacity to relinquish the need to control the other, to tolerate a sense of separateness and to understand how race has been and continues to be a vehicle that is used both consciously and unconsciously, for control and domination.

CHAPTER FOUR

Predicaments in practice

I n this chapter we include a number of shorter pieces about situations where professional guidelines were absent or in the process of change, and where the authors therefore had to find their own way out of their predicaments. There is a fine line between conventional professional behaviour and what we improvise when we find ourselves in uncharted territory. How to proceed without falling down and injuring ourselves, our patients or the reputation of our profession?

A London patient is sent by his employer to work elsewhere for 3 months. Whether and how to remain in contact whilst physically distant? A colleague is absent through illness – what do we do about that colleague's patients? A colleague, a friend, is dying, has died – what are the implications for those who undertake to help the patients through this time? Our own sell-by date is approaching – how do we face retirement?

Interestingly, acceptable and convenient practices were evolving even between the time we invited discussion and the date of this publication, as for instance, in the matter of "professional wills". Readers may nevertheless care to be reminded of the anxiety they may have experienced in similar circumstances, and there is much detail still to be considered.

Telephone work

Elizabeth Reddish

During the early Spring of last year I found myself marking out a 12-week period in my diary and at the same time each Monday evening I had a single patient's name in my diary. Nothing unusual in that, for this patient had been attending sessions for about two and a half years at this time. The difference was that for this period the once-weekly sessions were to be held on the telephone. To be more specific, they were to be conducted between my consulting room phone and a patient's mobile several hundred miles away.

I had never previously undertaken such a deviation of technique and quite apart from the challenge to the possibility of any psycho-analytic dimension to our proposed conversations, I was also aware of the fact that if the patient failed to call at the agreed time, it would leave me having to make a decision about whether to initiate contact myself. If I did so, apart from undertaking to bear the cost, I might find my patient too busy to talk at all or in the position of having to make me an offer of some kind: a different time, another day. But if I did not call, I might have to bear, possibly for weeks, not knowing why my patient had not called and therefore what state he might be in. The arrangement was full of potential holes that the absence of a proper setting would then make it impossible to make sense of, to either the patient or to myself. The potential hazards made it hard to warrant entering into this situation at all. But the alternative was to agree an absence of 12 weeks' duration and my countertransfer-ence feelings around this prospect were that the period might get infinitely extended. That is to say, there was a powerful, almost overwhelming sense of the need for regular, structured holding.

The patient did not request these sessions. My decision to offer them was premised on intuition about what might be best (includ-ing what might be the result of no contact), on pragmatism, taking into account what might be possible (for him and for me), but principally on a number of ideas I had about him and his state of mind as I had lately perceived it. As he was someone whose first line of defence against the perceived threat of "other people", that is, of relating in any meaningful way, had been since childhood to phantasize obsessively about suicide, I had always kept a focused eye on his experience of our relationship. Terrified of entrapment and tending to experience the potential of containment as a threat of incarceration, his mood in recent weeks had been less characterized by fear. An emergent capacity for reflection, for being able to be interested in, to think about his own beliefs and ideas, had recently caused him to comment: "I've realised I don't know what it's like to live with an idea that things *won't* go wrong". After witnessing for many months his fumbling around in a paranoid twilight, the clarity of this remark took me aback.

Having said this, something had happened about four weeks previously which had set me wondering if I had witnessed the first tentative reaching out to a different kind of object. On one occasion the patient had left his gloves on the chair in my room between sessions. It was not the leaving of the gloves so much as my counter-transference thoughts about the place in which the patient should re-discover them. I sensed there would be a critical difference between his finding them in exactly the same place as he left them or, say, simply on the table in the middle of the room, revealing that they had been moved. In the event I opted to have him re-discover them just where he had left them. I had held onto something for him, in his absence and kept it safe.

For quite a while he had been unable to use public transport, enter shops, or get his hair cut, but I began to notice a gradual relaxation. Having essentially been in a state of withdrawal from professional and social contact, and experiencing a depression that he told me was worse than any he'd previously experienced, there had been increasing evidence of a more hopeful capacity to stand up for himself, internally. He could more often and more vigorously be in a state of mind where he might say to himself "*I* do it like *this*", rather than be obsessed by thoughts such as "what are people thinking about me?" That is, there was tentative evidence of liberation from the rigid grip of paranoid anxiety in which he seemed to have been held for many years and which had brought him near to death a number of times.

The reason for the imminent three-month absence, which was

precipitating thoughts about if and in what form sessions could be maintained, was the significant fact that he felt able to work again after having been on long-term sick leave. This initiative therefore felt timely and hopeful within the context of his treatment, but he knew that he would straight away be seconded to work elsewhere.

In the event, the calls were held during the period of his usual session time, were between 25 and 35 minutes long and were initiated by the patient. They could not be described as "sessions" except to the extent that I was doing my best to bring my understanding of the patient to each encounter. In all cases the patient was standing outside in March and early April evenings, making me conscious of his physical discomfort. I did not at the time take up with him the conditions under which he chose to talk to me, beyond eliciting the information that he was indeed still working at this hour; implying that these were the only conditions under which contact could be maintained. Would it have felt too intimate or incarcerating to call from his hotel room? With hindsight I wonder whether the rigidity of my thinking around the times of the sessions had more to do with my own anxiety about diverting from psychoanalytic technique? At the same time something ever-present in my communications with this man was a sense that if structure was lost, *all* was lost. My dilemma was that to interpret this anxiety would be to threaten a psychic equilibrium that he struggled desperately to maintain. I had learnt from experience that one nudge in the wrong direction would cast him to the lions; he would become dominated by one of the most pernicious attacking and tormenting superegos I have ever experienced in my clinical practice and from which it could take him days or weeks to recover. The calls were cut short by the necessity of his returning to work but unconsciously, I believe what he was doing was "getting enough" to stabilize his state of mind (and no more).

Reflecting subsequently on how this series of conversations impacted on his treatment, I took note of a sentiment he expressed in his first session back in person which also just preceded the next analytic break. He talked about continuity and nurture and how he felt he needed these in his life now.

I believe that in formative childhood years my patient's experience of attempting to negotiate with his objects had been to stimulate their intrusion into, and invasion of, his mind. His experience of boarding school from an early age had been catastrophic, affording him an experience of primary objects as torturing and tormenting. His hopeful observation that "I no longer feel that everything is pre-set and that I have no authorship" suggested to me that my decision to maintain contact had been experienced by him as evidence of being with an object that offered a different kind of response. This man had felt compelled to kill off his objects just as he had experienced being killed off by them. His compulsive suicidal ideation was a defence; it kept him in a place where he could at least feel that he, rather than his object, would be the agent of his own demise. If this is correct, my response was clearly experienced by him as something new and qualitatively different. As such, this experience may have sown the seeds of psychic change.

When retirement threatens

Josephine Klein

This does not happen to everyone but it happens, I think, more often than people allow. Anyway, it happened to me. I realized I was not remembering as well as I used to. Sometimes there seemed a wall between me and an association just the other side of consciousness. A patient would speak with gratitude or reproach of what had gone on last Tuesday, and it was unavailable to me. Later, too late, the memory would return. Anxiety about not remembering made things worse, of course, but the failures could not be attributed solely to anxiety, nor, alas, to reverie. I had myself examined medically. Doctors were complimentary about my intellect, career, liveliness, etc., and said there was nothing wrong they could detect. I knew my memory was failing. Friends and colleagues to whom I mentioned it also declared they had noticed nothing wrong. However, after two years of this, I realized I must not take on new patients.

Looking back now, more than ten years later, I have to say that because one has to look so far ahead, it is very easy to postpone this decision of not taking on new patients. Yet one does not know in advance how long a patient will take. Patients training to be therapists are in a particularly vulnerable position. It may quite possibly take them ten years from start to finish. And training-therapists are supposed to be role models, careful to work at a high standard so that the student's temptation to laxity or complexity or mechanical interpretation, or other faults, finds no support from how their therapist treated them. Certainly I, by the time I had exhausted the resources of medical investigation, self-analysis, and friends' opinions, could not be sure that I still had ten years of good self-disciplined practice before me. No more patients, I decided, certainly no more therapists in training. One of my more difficult tasks was to warn a very promising patient, who was hoping to train in a couple of years, that I would not then be available, and that we should consider ending the therapy so as to leave ample time for the switch to a new therapist.

The prospect of not practising psychotherapy any more was very painful to me. Theories of dynamics and of technique were changing so beguilingly for the better, I was longing to work with it all. Anna Freud and Dorothy Burlingham, among others, practised into their nineties, said my more megalomaniac self, why could not I? I felt very isolated in this distress since no one would acknowledge it with me. There was a general unconscious conspiracy of denial, and several people of my own age and older, whose work I judged to be, from what they said about it, not so very wonderful, would come up to me and tell me how well they were coping, and *they* were not giving up, not they. At which times I would feel I could do murder.

In retrospect, I am astonished at how natural I had thought it that I should not retire. And that seems endemic in our professional culture: doctors retire, engineers retire, academics retire, but not we; they know that inevitably new ideas and new techniques will overtake them, which they will be slow to absorb, but not I. I took it for granted that I would see patients as long as I was alive.

I ask myself, was I fortunate or unfortunate in knowing that I was not as alert as I had been? What about people who are less conscious that their powers are declining, who may be confronted by a sudden revealing incident? And, indeed, what about our patients? I at least had years to get used to the idea of my decline, and a chance to adapt gradually and find enough other satisfactions to compensate for the pain of giving up clinical work.

As is generally known, but hard to accept if it comes before one is emotionally ready, there are all sorts of implications to retirement:

financial, social, domestic. Ten years from first realization to the fateful moment is not too long a time to achieve a tolerable alternative to work one loves. I am grateful that I saw it coming, that I am of a tolerably stoic disposition, and had alternative ways of being to which I could, at the least, resign myself. Though it took pretty well ten years to get to that state of mind. Looking back I am glad I had the foresight.

It would be impertinent for me to advise others on how to survive successfully into the more retired state. But I do think that it takes years. Should the L.C.P. Institute give an automatic "nudge" at 65? I am told that the Institute of Psycho-Analysis used routinely to send its members a fine bouquet at 65, to intimate that they should retire. Perhaps this is an "urban myth". But I wonder – should a letter be sent to everyone at 65, setting out some of the decisions which may need to be faced some time soon? Perhaps this is approaching the thing too bureaucratically. Perhaps what is needed is a Retiring Members group, membership of which is automatic when a person reaches 65 (60? 70?): a sort of L.C.P. of the Third Age. Nothing compulsory. It would not require people to have retired, or to have applied to belong, but it would be an acknowledgement that they have moved into that phase of the professional life cycle where it is realistic to consider implications and possibilities. Who can tell what such a group might achieve?

On the sudden death of a therapist

Prophecy Coles

I have twice had the painful experience of dealing with patients whose therapist died unexpectedly. One therapist died in the middle of a day's work, and had seen patients an hour or two before his death. The other therapist had died during a holiday break. Neither of them had made provision for such an event. And therefore the first thing I learned was that it is absolutely essential that we all make a will, a list of the patients we bequeath to trusted colleagues and friends in case of our sudden death. This is an essential part of good practice and our will needs to be updated every six months.

The next point I would make is that in my experience, it is

important to have not one but two or three friends who will take up one's patient list. I took on the entire list of ten patients for one colleague, in a moment of grief and panic, and I would have done better if I had been able to share the work. How I dealt with this list was to offer all the patients the chance of meeting me and talking about the death. Five took this opportunity, and I offered them up to four "bereavement sessions". Of the five I saw, three went on into another therapy. Of the five I did not see, three requested that they be referred direct to another therapist. From my experience of the two deaths, I think it might be expected that from any practice at least half will want to continue in therapy.

As one thinks about the friends and colleagues one will ask to carry one's list, I think it might be important to bear in mind that one may be leaving behind a partner or spouse who has come to know and have a feel for one's case load. The bereaved partner may need some sort of contact, if only to know that the patients are managing as well as may be. So my suggestion is that we leave our list with colleagues and friends who know one's partner, and might be prepared to keep contact for a little time.

In both the situations in which I was concerned, many patients wanted to come to the cremation or the memorial service. Appropriate information was provided, and many came. I also gave explicit details of the nature of the therapists' deaths. I felt that this would make the mourning process easier.

I took on one patient from each therapist's list. The experience of taking over a patient from a friend or a colleague is a strange one: to some extent the therapy is bound to be affected. The dead therapist is alive in one's mind, and has a place in one's own internal furniture, and this adds a twist to the therapy. The patient and I shared someone we had both known. At the anniversary of the therapist's death I was processing my own mourning as well as thinking about the patient's grief, and I had to be more than usually observant that I was not imposing my own emotions on the material. More difficult still was the breakdown of privacy. One can seem like a voyeur as one learns about the experience that the patient had with the dead therapist. One may find oneself stepping in the footsteps of a much-loved therapist who has left a patient deeply traumatized by the death. This can be hard to bear and think about. For instance I would have defensive thoughts along the line of "Oh come, it's not as bad as all that; there are other therapists in the world". And then, as one learns about the dead therapist's working habits, one can feel one should not be hearing these things. If the therapist had a technique very different from one's own, one can feel critical or even shocked. Sometimes the critical anger may be one's own grief and anger at the death, and one may find oneself wanting to blame the therapist for dying. At other times, one can feel one could never measure up to the skill and imagination of the dead therapist.

To end on a more positive note. One patient said to me that one way she had come to think of her therapist was to imagine that he had taken her along a path, but he could not take her any further. She felt that I was not a replacement for him, and as I was not, I was able to give her a different experience – one that she would not have been able to have with him.

Staying well

Jennifer Silverstone

"Illness is the night-side of life, a more onerous citizenship. Everyone who is born holds dual citizenship, in the kingdom of the well and in the kingdom of the sick. Although we all prefer to use only the good passport, sooner or later each of us is obliged at least for a spell, to identify ourselves as citizens of that other place."

Sontag, 1978, p. 3

Therapists have an obligation to stay well for their patients, to provide a safe space where work can be done, and to make provision for their patients if they are unavoidably absent, ill, or indeed die. Therapists too have an obligation to be vigilant about their own capacity for mental functioning. For this we need our colleagues and institutions to help us make the painful and difficult decisions to take time off for illness, for difficult life events, or to face retirement from our professional lives. Therapists in private practice are now required to keep sealed lists of their patients lodged with at least two colleagues, and in turn their colleagues' names are placed within our institutions. This is a recent improvement in practice designed to help others to locate the patients of the absent therapist and in turn find therapists who can be available for the patients who may need holding in the kind of emergency that results in the sudden and unavoidable disappearance of their therapist.

Absences that come about when the therapist is pregnant have been more frequently documented than the ones brought about by illness and death. Pregnancy is not on the whole thought about as pathology and therapists have become more open about, and interested in, the dynamics between them and their patients when a pregnancy has been announced. Illness and absences of other kinds are more open to being analysed, thought of as pathology, or criticized for being selfish or unnecessary. A therapist needs to be robust and reliable not just in their own mind, but considered to be so by his or her colleagues in order to gain referrals and to maintain their status in the community. It is not surprising that there be some reluctance to discuss illness. A feature of pregnancy unique in the life cycle is its potential for predictability. Nine months are set aside with the clear goal of achieving a live mother and infant and it is increasingly possible for women to plan the timing of the onset of pregnancy. However pregnancy raises a distinct set of issues, primarily the issue of management: when to inform the patient about the pregnancy, and whether to inform patients of the safe arrival of the baby; when to stop work; and when to return to practice after the baby is born. Most pregnant therapists experience pregnancy as a state of well-being and do not fear either for their lives or for their capacity to resume their work, but being pregnant arouses complex questions in the internal world of both the patients and the therapist. Therapists have to encounter pre-natal fears, "The general contention in the literature on the subject is that the analyst's pregnancy intensifies the transference and the counter-transference and that it tends to disturb technical neutrality" (Etchegoyen, 1993, p. 141). Etchegoyen emphasizes the need to stay firmly within analytic boundaries and to stay in regular supervision to be robust enough to face the fears and anxieties which the pregnancy in her case aroused, and work them through in order to be free to take on the various projections of her patients. Deben-Mager (1993, p. 138) in discussing successive pregnancies and the disruption they cause writes about the increased capacity for acting out:

> An analyst's pregnancy intensifies the transference and requires from the patient the capacity to experience the intensity of the

evoked feeling. Accordingly acting out is shown to be more vehement in the course of both pregnancies. [Deben-Mager, 1993, p. 138]

Mariotti (1993) in thinking around countertransference responsiveness also discusses pre-natal fears and here the discussion is pertinent to other states of mind in the therapist. For what prevents this therapist from disclosing her state of being pregnant to the patient is her own anxiety; she dare not disclose her condition until and unless the issues of foetal abnormality and the viability of the pregnancy are resolved.

> I am trying to convey a general impression of the feelings my patients brought into the consulting room when they did not know what was happening – something from which they were excluded, that was frightening and forbidden, and even dangerous to know, or impossible to understand with reason and to which one could only react with an action. The anxiety of not knowing, wanting to know and being afraid, the sense of forbidden knowledge, to which others have access and not oneself . . . When eventually the time came to let them know, some of the deeper anxieties were relieved, but not surprisingly, new ones arose. [Mariotti, 1993, p. 154]

Though this discourse is around pregnancy it serves well to describe the unconscious communication between patient and therapist when illness or personal disturbance cannot be disclosed.

Gottleib (1989) points out that pregnancy can be "a potent transference stimulus" and suggests that

> the pregnant therapist can provide a focus for what is perhaps the most primitive phantasy of all: a harmonious existence in a merged state of unity with the all-providing mother where frustration, anger and grief have no place and a truly perfect mother is the infant's exclusive property. [Gottleib, 1989, p. 294]

All these papers take into account the state of mind of the therapist in the grips of the bodily changes and excitations of the pregnancy and the consequences of these feelings as they affect themselves and their patients. Pregnant therapists have to manage a shift in concern from being wholly engaged with the mind of the patient to being drawn into primary maternal preoccupation and all the inward turning-in of the psyche that that state of mind demands.

> For some women, pregnancy may be one of the most enriching stages of the life cycle . . . a young woman whose experience with her own mother has been "good enough", the temporary regression to a primary identification with the omnipotent, fertile, life-giving mother, as well as with herself as if she were her own child; is a pleasurable developmental phase in which further maturation and growth of the self may be achieved. For other women, the inevitable regression occasioned by pregnancy and motherhood may be a painful and frightening experience. [Pines, 1982, p. 311]

Pines is here discussing patients but it is clear that both these frames of mind will be to some extent apparent in the pregnant therapist. All the papers mentioned here discuss the complexities and desirability of retaining the analytic stance in the face of the changing external reality, the therapist's obviously changed physical state, and the recognition that symbolically and literally there is another in the consulting room. Likewise what has to be taken into account in the reality of a pregnancy is the painful recognition that a pregnancy requires a two-person relationship and this reality drags the therapist into an inevitable if not overtly revealed relationship with an other.

The pregnant therapist will struggle both with her own regression and an anticipated excitement of a new maturity which mothering may bring in its wake. The therapist who has been pregnant returns to work, having taken time away from patients, and struggles with the conflicting demands of family and work. Her health if not jeopardized, during the pregnancy is not in question, she is not vulnerable in that way. She is free to pick up the rivalries and fears, attacks envious and otherwise of her patient, she is free to take on referrals and continue to work, still experienced by her colleagues as competent and undamaged by the experiences she has had.

The therapist faced with illness will only be subject to painful regression, for though there is secondary gain in illness the fear in a reasonably well analysed therapist will outweigh the temporary secondary gains of illness; furthermore there is no certainty of outcome, and only in some circumstances might there be personal growth.

It is no easy task to return to the workplace in which one's immediate needs have absolutely no outlet for expression, after one has spent a prolonged period of time during which one's immediate needs were the primary focus of his attention and the attention of everyone around him. The obvious danger is that the analyst will use the patient for some of these regressive purposes. [Lasky, 1990, p. 465]

In my experience of having two ill therapists in supervision the task became one of helping them to leave their practice with all the pain of separation and mourning that that entailed as they faced the terminal nature of their illnesses.

Physical illness and bodily injury inevitably undermine one's sense of identity, interrupt the secure indwelling in one's body and may lead to emotional regression. As a consequence a reorganisation is required on the physical, emotional and cognitive planes. This process is often slow, difficult and painful. [Durban *et al.*, 1993, p. 703]

It is possible that sick therapists can be more in touch with their own vulnerability and more attuned to the precarious nature of life, and less inclined to make promises to patients, internally debated and externally declared that cannot be fulfilled. These may be along the lines of omnipotent statements such as, "I will always be here for you" and more in touch with the ability not to reassure either themselves or their patients for reassurance sake. There is a profound challenge in the work when endings have to be faced and there is a struggle with the wish to regress into the self and the equally demanding wish to be available and lively of mind for the therapeutic work; however it is clear that splitting and denial are close to the surface of the ill therapist's mind. A capacity to deny the sick part of the self may need to be exploited in order to be free to work, but there is a tension between the denial and the wish to integrate the ill self with the healthy. Staying with illness when there is a lively wish for life is a challenge not just to the therapists, but also to those involved in their supervision and support of a more general kind.

The sick therapist is still a container for the patient, still working and dealing with the central theme of separation and loss. Central to the ideas of analytic neutrality are the ideas of analytic privacy, and what in their paper Durban *et al.* (1993) call the "cracked container".

> Essentially we describe a "cracked container" in two senses of the term. Firstly the body, which was supposed to be an unobtrusive partner in our work, has, literally, become an irritant and a saboteur. Secondly this difficult and painful confrontation with the limits of our ability will be experienced as a crack in the therapeutic function of containing. The therapist's private psychic contents, which should have remained self-contained have leaked out uncontrollably. The illness as an excess of reality permeates the therapeutic space. [Durban *et al.*, 1993, p. 708]

It is not only illness that takes us away from the consulting room; therapeutic work is punctuated by other absences. We all take breaks, for the holidays, and for events in our lives that require our presence outside the consulting room. All breaks in continuity create spaces for the interpretation of feelings that are aroused by absence. Patients may and do struggle with the rigour of our timetable, and we are familiar with the anger that the imposition of our timetable creates, so it is no wonder that we are often reluctant to take time off for our own needs. As Gottleib (1989) points out having taken a shorter period of maternity leave than she may have needed, she then discovered that "returning to work with a small baby proved considerably harder than working whilst pregnant".

Some years ago a colleague became ill with a rare disease that was to kill her within three years. She was working in private practice and had various commitments in the wider psychotherapeutic community as a supervisor both privately and within local institutions. Her illness was not a straightforward one and she was initially misdiagnosed, but she made a brief recovery, a kind of remission from the disease. At the onset of her illness she had, with the help of her own supervisor, organized a hospital stay, and then a return to work. During the next two and half years she worked as hard as ever and, though limiting her travelling commitments, she continued to travel to courses where she supervised and taught. Her health was closely monitored and she was in touch with her colleagues, and was in personal supervision, as well as working for counselling services and supervising counsellors. For this therapist it was possible that she had the time to get to know her illness as she lived with it, thought about it and internalized it, and as Durban *et al.* talk about she "befriended" it.

> When working when physically ill, the therapist needs to befriend his illness, to get to know it from a certain distance, to become acquainted with it. This acknowledgement enables an awareness of the limitations illness generates, without turning the patient into an active partner in it. [Durban *et al.*, 1993, p. 708]

For this therapist her illness had to be acknowledged and worked with and faced. It was clear when we spoke to her patients later that for some of them valuable and deeply containing work was achieved whilst acknowledging this painful reality of her mortality.

A year into her recovery she was able to talk to another colleague who had had cancer and who was concerned about the strain of working with patients while under the threat of her recurring illness. They spoke together and found it supportive. Sometime later they were both prepared to share their insights with a peer group and presented an evening on the theme of being therapists coping with their own illnesses. These therapists were faced in their work by patients with similar symptoms and vulnerabilities closely linked with their own, and they found that patients who shared with their therapist their symptoms, unconscious terror and fear of death were offered a deep unconscious mutuality. The ill therapist has to be able to contain for these patients not just the empathic response to illness but the capacity to contain the patient's recovery whilst dealing with any envy and ambivalence that their patient's recovery might arouse.

> When the analysand discovers through experience that the analyst is receiving the transference via his own inner life, however distressing, in order to understand his patient's communications more fully, in that moment he realizes that both he and his analyst share the self-analytic function. [Bollas, 1987, p. 255]

There is a constant need for the therapist's self-analysis in order to address the question as to whether our own symptoms are neurotic, or are old but freshly awakened unconscious terrors. What do we experience as acceptable in our ability to tolerate exhaustion, pain and backache? What symptoms should be analysed, what should go to the GP? When should we be at work, and when should we take time off to rest and heal? In one form or another each of us in the group asked similar questions of ourselves, ducked the issues, or reluctantly faced them. What about projections, identification, patients who make you feel ill, those patients who unconsciously know you to be ill, and those who have your disease in another form?

The group spoke about our wish to be omnipotent around the realities of human illness and frailty. This omnipotence is revealed in our reluctance to seek medical help, in our resistance to taking time off away from the consulting room and our belief that we may find the cure through our own self-analysis. It is a hard task to watch for the internal retreat of the individual therapist caught in the web of illness. We are used to watching vigilantly for illness in our patients, sometimes in a punitive way. We interpret resistance and look out for somatizing, sometimes without due care to the organic. All patients miss sessions, and illnesses have to be thought about and open to interpretation, but we wondered whether our own weaknesses are denied and re-presented as omnipotent coping. Double the internal work is required both to acknowledge one's vulnerability and re-work it in order to continue to be for the patient a containing object. The therapist wishes to stay alive and work. We cannot make this assumption on behalf of the patient nor on behalf of the therapist whose illness is taking them towards death. Those colleagues whose illness took a firm hold of them ceased to work, but they did not wish for death in an instinctual sense but rather they returned to what Winnicott (1988b) refers to as the "state of aloneness of pre-dependence, since this has been experienced".

Some time elapsed and the therapist left a note on her consulting room door, ordered a taxi and went into hospital. She never recovered. She had left a list of all her patients' names, addresses and telephone numbers and by some of them a brief note, sometimes a sketch of history, or a note about the referrer. She also left a note of the name of a colleague and supervisor. We were able to get the details of this list over the telephone from a family member and we decided that our function would be two-fold: to deal with the patients of a desperately ill therapist and to release the family from any burden of responsibilities a dying therapist might have. We roughly split the patient group to share the task and were then faced with the difficulty of deciding how best to contain them, with little information as to how the illness would develop, whether it would be fatal, or whether the therapist herself would be able to say goodbye to some of them.

We sat together making the calls alternately, so being able to learn from each other how to manage each patient's response and how best to contain their anxiety whilst communicating uncertainty. The thought that went into the task was one of management and of holding the boundaries. Management for us meant clearly addressing the states of mind and feelings which would be unleashed in patients faced with the crisis of losing their therapist. Holding the boundary also meant working in a way that would keep the therapist whole and intact for the possibly grieving, angry and distressed patient. We decided that we would offer to keep the patients informed of their therapist's progress on a weekly basis. That meant giving them our telephone numbers and offering to call back ourselves. We also decided to offer the ones who seemed overwhelmingly distressed the opportunity of a one-off session to talk about their feelings about their ill therapist, but not to do any other work with them. The ones who felt that if their therapist did not recover they would need anyway to go and continue therapy were eventually referred on.

We were able to contact almost all of the patients. One or two of them clearly needed to be seen promptly and took up the offer; others, we felt, were relieved simply to know that someone would be available. Others could be held by phone calls and the promise that someone (i.e. one of us,) was there for them and would keep them informed. Throughout this process we felt how important it was that the boundaries should be held and that as fellow therapists we could and did hold them. It involved us in a lot more work. The phone calls took time and although the offer of our availability was enough for many of the patients, four were seen. Referrals on to colleagues were also done by telephone. There was no possibility of the therapist becoming in her absence anyone other than the patient's therapist – a boundary that a family member would find impossible to hold. We were able to keep patients away from the hospital and the home and to offer them an opportunity to express their rage and anger as well as their sadness. We felt too that we had become a bridge for the family to express their feelings about a loved mother with a separate and professionally valued life.

Within three weeks of her hospital admission the therapist had died. With foresight she had arranged a funeral, which was to be open to anyone who wanted to attend. As Lasky (1990, p. 456) points out, "I think that an analyst who has never contemplated his mortality, and who has never set into place any mechanisms for the management of his practice should anything happen to him, is engaging in a form of denial". After the service only family and friends and colleagues were invited to meet together. The therapist left instructions that her clinical notes be destroyed. Neither my colleague nor I had worked so closely together before attending the business of a very ill colleague. We both felt we had learned a lot and shared a deep experience. We felt we had done all we could do for the patients and indeed all we could for a colleague. It made us aware that to be clear about our own capabilities and boundaries it is important to keep up to date lists of patients in treatment to make sure that someone other than a family member a colleague knows what to do when we are ill or absent. It seems clear that our responsibilities as therapists are with us even when we are ill and as part of our responsibilities to our patients it seems right that we make provision for our absence; and even provision for our death. (I am aware that this is now a formal obligation on all therapists, but at the time this was not common practice.) It felt to us that, freed from the intimacy of being a family member, staying in the role of colleague rather than friend enabled us to continue in the therapeutic stance, which ultimately helped the patients to mourn a dead therapist, someone who in absence and illness had become too vulnerable to mourn and express anger with. Perhaps what now seems the most important aspect of the work was the holding of the therapeutic stance for an ill colleague.

Absences cannot be avoided, but they can be creatively used. Envy and hostility can be aroused: fear of loss of the other, being absent when needed, being lost in the mind of the other is familiar analytic territory. Some sessions are missed by the patient to test out the validity of being held in mind. Just as patients envy their analyst's freedom, life and imagined fulfilments, analysts can, and indeed do, envy their patients, their freedom, their capacity to get well and to leave them and to have their own particular joys. I think that we may in our interpretation of absences underestimate our patient's capacities for understanding and empathy, and for the development of authentic concern for another which can enrich the work and give it deeper meaning. In a long analysis elements of the life cycle are experienced in reality as well as worked through in the retrieval and understanding of the past; the unconscious made conscious, birth, life and death, come and go in the material, but they are also present in the real life of the patient and the analyst. There is a sense of loss and a possible guilt or shame in leaving our patients, however temporarily, as well as a relief. Understanding and empathic response can go both ways in the consulting room as long as the boundaries are clear. The analytic couple may indeed struggle with absence, but there is always a possibility that both may emerge the stronger.

CHAPTER FIVE

The pregnant therapist

Sue Gottlieb

Introduction

T he pregnant woman cannot fail to evoke powerful feelings in all around her; whether such feelings are denied or embraced, she calls forth a complex and varying mixture of delight, concern, fear and disgust, along with envy of her capacity to conceive and bear a baby, and jealousy of the baby in its phantasized state of uterine bliss. I would like to consider what happens to her analytic practice when she is a psychoanalytic therapist.

The emotions and ideas evoked by pregnancy might be normal grist for the analytic mill were it not for the fact that the therapist's pregnancy itself constitutes such an intrusion into the analytic setting as it has been established. Not only will the usual open-ended continuity be interrupted by maternity leave and perhaps by unforeseen complications, but also, and more importantly, pregnancy breaches the usual degree of analytic anonymity by bringing the personal life of the therapist right into the therapy in a particularly dramatic way. Uniquely, a third person – the unborn baby – is physically present in the consulting room, and pregnancy is an unmistakeable "admission" of sexual activity and a statement about a relationship to a man and a family. In a sense, the patient suffers the loss of an illusion – an illusion fostered to some degree by the protected analytic setting – that the therapist exists only in her consulting room and only in relation to the patient.

Of course, in normal circumstances the patient is always being presented with clues to the therapist's separate existence. The existence of breaks and gaps underline her "other life" away from the patient, the presence of sibling-patients remind the patient that she is by no means his or her exclusive possession, and in her very capacity to think independently the therapist is always, from the patient's perspective, potentially part of an excluding couple (Britton, 1989). Most patients come to know various things about her professional and private life outside the consulting room, and how the patient construes what he or she "knows" is always having to be picked up in the therapy. But pregnancy is different, in that it confronts the patient so directly and bluntly with the fact that his or her therapist is an actively sexual woman with a personal life which takes place outside the control of the patient. It is this uncompromising confrontation with the sexuality of the therapist which marks pregnancy out from other "special events" (Weiss, 1975) which occur in a therapy, such as the therapist becoming ill or moving. In the black and white world of primitive phantasy, the "madonna"-like mother who had seemed to be the infant's ever-available exclusive possession is rather shockingly revealed as the "whore"-like depriving mother who betrays the infant to sleep with her husband.

The process of coming to terms with the separateness of one's loved object is the very essence of the analytic work, but in the normal course of a therapy the patient can at least proceed at his or her own pace. The patients of a pregnant therapist rather have the facts forced upon them, whether or not they are ready, in much the same way that a child may have to accommodate to the birth of a younger sibling before he or she is ready to be weaned (in the widest sense of the word.) Whether or not the therapist's pregnancy *does* interfere with the natural course of the therapy, it will certainly be experienced as a potentially catastrophic rupture in maternal containment. This is because the analytic setting – by which I mean the analytic mode of listening, the way that the therapist concerns herself with the patient without requiring the patient to be concerned with her in the same way, and the way that she protects the work from external interruptions or distractions – is itself experienced as a form of of maternal containment, and so any disruption in the consistency of this "atmosphere of safety" will feel like an abandonment by the therapist-mother of her patient-baby.

As long as she can maintain her analytic function, the patients of a pregnant therapist have a rich opportunity to work through the feelings evoked by pregnancy at first hand, but the difficulties involved, for patient and therapist, should not be underestimated (Lax, 1969; Breen, 1977; Barbanel, 1980; Clementel-Jones, 1985; Fenster *et al.*, 1986; Gottlieb, 1989; Wedderkopp, 1990; Deben-Mager, 1993; Etchegoyen, 1993; Mariotti, 1993). I think it does require a certain amount of determination for a patient to carry on with the therapy under difficult circumstances and, for her part, the pregnant therapist is required to contain her patient's intense feelings of disturbance and protect the analytic setting whilst she herself is in a unique state of emotional and physical vulnerability. In my view the "real" trauma for the patient, which may not be survivable, would be the loss by the therapist of her analytic function.

In this paper I would like to expand on the nature of the disruption to the normal analytic setting and consider its effect on the analytic process itself. I base my remarks on my own experience of working through two pregnancies, two and a half years apart, some twenty years ago towards the end of my training and as a newly-qualified psychoanalytic psychotherapist. From this distance I can only indicate some of the themes and issues relating to my pregnancy, with brief clinical examples rather than an extensive report.

Some clinical themes

On becoming pregnant with my first child I was immediately confronted with the question of whether I should inform my patients (and, if so, when) or whether I should wait for them to notice in their own way and in their own time. I also had to think about how long a break to take and when to begin my maternity leave. To tell or not to tell seems to be a central issue for the pregnant therapist, and opinions are divided on whether to inform the patient. In my case I decided that I would tell my patients, and that I would do so when I was three months pregnant. My rationale in doing this was to allow plenty of time to work through the issues raised by the pregnancy and the break itself. On balance, I now believe that this decision was the product of my anxiety about being able to "hold" my analytic role because of my inexperience. I was also over-compensating for my own guilt about (as I felt) abandoning my patients for a long break and (as I felt) disrupting their therapy by imposing upon them such a provocative event of my own. These days I would favour waiting for the patient to recognize the pregnancy in his or her own way, rather than risk pre-empting a response by informing the patient. How and when the patient notices the pregnancy (or fails to) is very revealing of his or her way of functioning. Some will notice and ask a direct question, others (more frightened of their curiosity) will allude to it in a disguised way and the therapist will have to be alert to the patient's unconscious recognition and help bring it out into the open. If the patient is in such a state of denial as not to be able to take in the fact of the pregnancy for some while, the therapist is faced with the additional anxiety about running out of time as her maternity leave looms. She will have to take up the patient's difficulty in "seeing" what is now all too obvious, and she may eventually have to inform the patient rather than risk colluding with the denial.

The decision about *when* to tell the patient is interesting. I chose three months because this marked the time when I felt established enough in the pregnancy to be able to deal with my patients' reactions. What it means is that the pregnant therapist has to come to terms with her own pregancy before she can deal with the reactions of her patients. The issue is the same whether one informs the patient or not, because the patient may suspect the pregnancy before the therapist is ready to confirm it.

Miss L, for example, seemed to recognize my pregnancy at some unconscious level some while before I was ready to address her suspicions. When I was 10 weeks pregnant, she dreamed of going into a large dining hall where there had been a massacre of children. Horrible mutilations had taken place and everyone was very upset. She was taken into a small room and shown her handbag which had been neatly dissected. The top had been sliced off and she was invited to pull out the contents. She was reluctant to do so, for fear of finding bits of body. Someone removed from the handbag a plastic bag with what looked like chicken feet in it. She realized that it was a foetus in an amniotic sac. It became clear that she was responsible for murdering the children. She said that she had tried to tell people how much she wanted a child, but no one had listened. She had gone to a hospital and heard someone say "her breasts are full of milk". Parents now started arriving to pick up their children, as if from an adventure playground, and were devastated by the horrific scene. A man with a knife appeared and began slicing into his leg, in order to demonstrate to her what she had done to the children. In association she said that the knife revealed "what was inside".

This therapy was in its early stages and Miss L had become newly aware of her own wish for a sexual partner and a child. Both wishes had been long disavowed – all forms of need being equated with weakness – and although she was still of child-bearing age she was suffering deep regret about this area of her life having gone so wrong, as she felt. There are different ways of understanding the dream, but I was fairly sure that at one level it was about her unconscious recognition of my pregnancy. Certainly it expressed her intense wish for a child of her own – a wish that she had not been able to listen to until now – and her envy of parents with children. It contained her idea that she had tried to warn me about her murderous feelings towards my foetus, and because I couldn't listen to her she was driven to carry out these terrible acts. During the first three months of pregnancy a woman is usually self-absorbed and introspective in a particular way, and I think that although I was neither unwell with nausea nor especially "removed", Miss L was sensitive enough to pick up subtle changes in me, and to feel that I was "not listening" to her in my usual way.

Of course, it is impossible to know whether her dream *was* an implicit recognition of my pregnancy or not, but the point is that I did not feel free, at this early stage, to explore the possibility that it was. I was simply not ready to tell anyone outside my close family, or help anyone else with their feelings about my pregnancy. Instead I took up the dream's depiction of her murderous feelings towards the child (attachment seeking) part of her personality, and also her fear that my intention was to be so incisively knife-like in my analysis of her "insides" as to leave her neatly dissected with the top of her head sliced off and the contents of her mind pulled out. (In retrospect I can see that the attack upon her own child-like feelings would naturally be exacerbated by her sense that I was not listening to her.) The dream had a particularly disturbing quality, over and above the horror of the massacre, which possibly reflected Miss L's sense of being a child in the dark about what was going on in the mysterious adult world. Thrown back to the earliest anxieties about what goes on in a mother's body, it was as if she half-knew that *something* incomprehensible was going on, in me, which frightened and excluded her.

I was not free to explore the possibility that she thought I was pregnant because at that early stage I had not yet myself come to terms with my pregnancy. Birkstead-Breen (1986) suggests that the first months of pregnancy are full of "doubts, confusion, regrets, anxieties and disbelief" even when the baby is fully planned and joyfully anticipated. She points out that a woman is often afraid to acknowledge angry thoughts about the baby, even to herself, for fear that they can harm the child, and that the situation is aggravated by the fact that at this stage minimal medical reassurance is available concerning the baby. This is when the baby seems most at risk from the envious "evil eye", as shown by the numerous taboos about mentioning or noticing the pregnancy until it is advanced. If negative thoughts (from within or without) are felt to be such a danger to the baby, then it is difficult to meet the patient's intense hostility with the required neutral receptivity. Certainly I responded to Miss L's dream with intensely protective feelings towards my unborn baby.

The misgivings and disbelief of the first trimester of pregnancy usually give way to a new sense, in the second trimester, that the baby within is "real" and viable. Not long after Miss L's dream, at about 13 weeks, my internal state had changed and I felt fully available once again to receive projections and this was the point at which I felt ready for my patients to know that I was pregnant.

In the event, I did not tell all my patients in the way that I had planned. Miss A, for example, was only a few months into her therapy and it seemed that we were too close to a summer break. She had left a previous therapist following a summer break, and I was concerned that the therapy was not sufficiently established for it to survive the news of my pregnancy over a break. (Evidently, though I was ready for her to know, she was not, and in hindsight I would say that by holding back I was correctly responding to my unconscious knowledge that, in telling her, I would actually have been imposing information on her in a pre-emptive way.) On returning from the summer break, at which point I was nearly five months pregnant, she realized that I was pregnant. She simply asked me a direct question, and I confirmed that I was. Her immediate concern was whether I was going to give up work altogether, and I told her (as I did all my patients) that, barring complications, I planned to continue working until near my due date and to be on leave for eight weeks. (I took a maternity leave of four months when my second child was born, two and a half years later.) On this point, I think it is important to be as clear as possible about the *practical* consequences of the pregnancy, so that the boundaries of the therapy are protected and the emotional consequences of the pregnancy can best be contained and fully explored within the normal analytic setting.

With the pregnancy a "known fact", and with my patients reasonably reassured that it was at least my intention to carry on working, analytic work proceeded in this middle trimester in a reasonably "normal" way. There is a general consensus in the literature that, alongside sympathy and solicitude, the therapist's pregnancy will stir up feelings of sibling rivalry, envy, fear of abandonment, alternate idealization and denigration of the therapist, hostility towards the baby with consequent guilt feelings, and repugnance towards female sexuality – and so it was. Generally speaking, all my patients met my pregnancy with a degree of shock. Most expressed their pleasure and concern for me, all felt abandoned, excluded and disillusioned about the intrusion of *my* pregancy into *their* therapy. Of course, as one would expect, they reacted in their own particular way, in the light of their individual experience and according to their particular pattern of internal relationships. The transference issues that had already been a feature of each therapy were simply intensified.

Mrs F immediately dreamed of going to see "a therapist" in a hospital. She spent her "session" sitting in the waiting corridor while her therapist walked past her chatting to someone on the telephone. Clearly, she felt she had lost her lively connection with me as *"her* therapist" since I had, as she felt, turned away from her to the baby within me. I wondered if the telephone connection was like the umbilical cord linking me to my foetus, and I thought the dream showed not only how excluded she felt by my new relationship with my baby, but also how tantalizing it was for her. The "chatting" seemed to have rather a complacent, provocative quality as if I had become an object deliberately seeking to push feelings of exclusion into her. What had been "her" consulting room had turned into a "waiting corridor" in which she was forced to watch this rather sickening display of maternal devotion. Of course, I could not know, at this point, to what extent her picture of me chatting to my foetus was based on early experience of a rather infantile mother, say, who deliberately stirred up feelings of exclusion in her child, and to what extent her picture was a misrepresentation, distorted by envy. She had sought therapy for disturbing phantasies of strangling her young son when he cried, and these phantasies now pressed upon her in a nightmarish way. I understood them, like Miss L's dream, to express her wish to strangle anything baby-like, including the unborn baby to whom I was perpetually "on the telephone", as well as the crying baby within her. Not knowing how to attend to her feelings of deprivation, she thought her only option was the psychotic solution of killing off the baby part of her which generated the feelings. Her feeling that I was really rubbing her nose in the psychic "facts of life" (Money-Kyrle, 1971), in a most humiliating way, emerged even more clearly in a subsequent series of recurrent dreams in which she was a small child in bed with her parents. While they endlessly engaged in various forms of violent intercourse, she was left excluded, bewildered, excited and disgusted. In this climate of mindlessness I was encouraged by signs of a genuine wish, on her part, to comprehend what had happened to me (and think about what was happening to her) but it caused her great anxiety. A dream about a small child insistently and furtively putting her hand up Mrs F's skirt seemed to depict her own life-giving curiosity as a furtive and essentially disgusting intrusiveness which could only annoy me.

Miss A similarly believed that I was deserting her in order to replace her with a baby, perhaps never to return. Her central object relationship was with an internal mother who seemed just too tired and preoccupied with other children to be sufficiently available to Miss A, and now she began a long period of mourning. In her poignant depression she felt lifeless, empty and tired, as if a vital link between us had been severed, and she remembered similar feelings when her mother went away with a "nervous breakdown" after the birth of a younger brother. She was distressed to discover how violently angry she was, with me and my baby. She was horrified by her wish to scratch me and kick me in the stomach. She dreamed of an appalling and frightening "big black sticky mess" on a beach, approached only by a steep and very difficult cliff path. She joined others on the cliff top who were running back in terror from what they had glimpsed. The mess seemed to represent her newly discovered well of anger and jealousy, hitherto so difficult to access and so terrifying for her to deal with. She was sure that I wanted to replace her with a "real" baby because she was so bad. The baby, on the other hand, would be able to love me uncritically and make me feel like a really good mother. She was also afraid that I would not be able to differentiate various negative feelings from one another, and that I would quickly label anything she did as a sign of her hostility rather than try to assess different sorts of motivation. Later she felt sure that the anger had been hidden away for so long that it had now "gone bad" within her, as though rotten and poisonous, and surrounding her with a "bad smell". In this state of mind the black mess within seemed to have taken on a more bitterly envious quality. At other times she likened it to a patch of tooth decay, spreading painfully; a formulation which stressed the almost unbearable nature of the pain she felt. She drew a painful contrast between us: where I had a receptive space filled with a live baby, she felt only emptiness within her; a "hole" which would now surely be filled with cancer.

The dream indicates how frightened Miss A was to let me see her black feelings – a mixture of depression, anger and envy – and how fearful she was of harming me. Generally speaking, my pregnancy made this depressive conflict especially acute for all patients. But whilst on the one hand my pregnancy evoked great rage (about deprivation) and envy, it also evoked a tender concern for me, along with the anxiety and anger that I would be too vulnerable to receive such feelings.

What my pregnancy seemed to activate most powerfully for all patients was a phantasy of an ideal state: a place in Paradise where ideal mother and ideal baby are linked together in perfect union. In this longed-for and idealized state of togetherness, the unborn baby is imagined as existing harmoniously in a merged state of unity with an all-providing mother. Frustration, anger and grief have no place, and a truly perfect mother is felt to be the infant's exclusive and continuous property. Correspondingly, the mother is felt to be so entirely satisfied by her infant as not to have any needs for another relationship. Of course, running counter to this phantasy is the fear of total loss of separate identity, expressed in feelings of suffocation and restriction.

Miss A, for example, projected herself into my *in-utero* baby and experienced a kind of bliss. She spoke of needing me to "connect" her, as if joined to me by an umbilical cord. She felt like a balloon which would "float around haphazardly" unless she were "grounded" by the string attached to me. On her own, "making connections" would be "like trying to thread a needle by holding the cotton too far from the end". There was a "direct link" between us which, she felt, allowed her to tell me things without conscious intervention. On a more conscious level she daydreamed about being my tiny baby, pushed in a pram and given my exclusive, undivided attention. In this phantasy I became very idealized but the idealization was not always of the same kind. Sometimes it was of a more "normal" and touching kind which allowed the phantasy to have a more reparative function – as if she could allow herself a new experience of being properly contained by a mother who wanted to take her in, at other times it had a more defensive flavour. She had, as it were, taken refuge from the blackness and fear of harming me in a daydream about getting inside the ideal mother.

In this mode the phantasy functioned as a kind of psychic retreat (Steiner, 1993), shutting out the converse experience of me in the transference as the negligent mother who was depriving and excluding her. She contrasted the "soft, caring light" in my consulting room with the "harsh, cold light" she could see coming from another room. I became a person with limitless supplies with whom she could merge, so doing away with all separateness. Merging (through projective identification) with the idealized "soft, caring" object-who-has-everything produces an experience of bliss because it magically erases all need and all humiliating difference. I think it had become terribly important for Miss A to hold on to this phantasy of blissful union because it helped her avoid what was otherwise a persecutory feeling of being in need. To make demands always faced her with an exhausted internal mother with limited resources complaining about her demands and making her feel awful about being a nuisance, and so the state of being in need had acquired a persecutory quality. When she could not hold on to the daydream of merger she was confronted with the painful internal reality of her relationship with this "harsh, cold" object.

As my pregnancy advanced into the third trimester, I had to think about how to handle the break itself; my primary concern being how best to protect the analytic setting given the unpredictable nature of childbirth. I was careful to set a well-defined ending date, in fairness to myself and my patients. I decided that, barring unforeseen complications, I would stop work three weeks before my due date because I felt that for my own sake I needed to be able to withdraw and become preoccupied with my baby. For my patients the clear ending date would, I hoped, offer some relief from the sense of unpredictability, and yet also assert the reality of the forthcoming separation. I considered that not to set a date would have been a form of denial on my part, as if encouraging patients to think that perhaps after all there was not really going to be an interruption or a baby. I also set the date on which I planned to resume work, with the proviso that I would of course let them know if I was not able to start work on the planned resumption date.

A related issue I considered at this point was whether I would give patients any further information and how I would handle questions when work resumed. Again, opinions are divided on this issue. Some therapists report sending a card or even telephoning the patient to announce the birth (Deben-Mager, 1993) but this would have been inconsistent with my normal analytic reserve. As Lasky (1990) points out, in his detailed consideration of what information he felt it right to give patients following his severe, sudden illness, what a therapist does in these extraordinary circumstances depends upon his or her theory of the analytic process. If one believes that the patient must be given the freedom to project his subjective internal world into the analytic situation (so forming the transference), then one will arrive at Lasky's view that whilst, clearly, he had to give his patients *some* information he believed it important to preserve as much anonymity as possible by giving as little factual information as possible. I too believe that simply answering questions (in the normal social way) about my health, the sex of the baby and so on, rather than taking up their particular meaning for the patient, would be inappropriately self-revealing and spell a breakdown in my analytic function. Of course, analysing rather than answering is by no means "the equivalent of making believe that nothing has happened (or is happening) between patient and analyst" (Lasky, 1990, p. 460).

With the break in view (some two months hence) the analytic work moved into a different phase. For the pregnant woman, the last trimester is about the preparation for birth (Birkstead-Breen, 1986; Raphael-Leff, 1980, 1993), and my patients were correspondingly full of associations to the unpredictable, fearful, but exciting nature of childbirth. This was when patients were most concerned about my vulnerability, a phantasy given added life on those occasions when I was fatigued and uncomfortable. Would their "bad feelings" make me go into labour prematurely, or give birth to a "monster", would I die in labour, would I (after all) want to stay with the baby and not come back to work? Would I come back the same person? Birkstead-Breen (1986) suggests that as time inexorably ticks by, unbearably quickly and unbearably slowly, the inevitable progression towards birth is like the inevitable progression towards death. One knows that it *will* surely happen, but *how* it will happen cannot be predicted. As my maternity leave loomed, the feeling of imminent separation was ever-present. In the last week or so, the sense of time running out had so intensified that most patients wished, to some extent and with varying degrees of success, to cut off from their feelings of loss. Miss L wanted to "cauterize" her feelings, as if bleeding – a word redolent of vaguely sinister surgical procedures she imagined me to be undergoing; Miss A wished she could leave therapy (in the hope that she could get away from her feelings of rejection by leaving them in me); and Mrs F was "mystified" about why she should attend her final few sessions, when all she could anticipate was the pain of loss being inflicted upon her – from her perspective a pain which served no good purpose at all.

Discussion

Pregnancy is certainly a special event, as Weiss (1975) termed "anything which alters or intrudes upon the basic analytic situation", such as meetings between patient and therapist which take place outside the consulting room, and the therapist's illness or lateness. Many of these intrusions, as in the case of pregnancy, are due to a change in the therapist's life circumstances and they cause some or other aspect of the therapist's personal life to be suddenly and unexpectedly revealed. They inevitably cause a sense of shock, and a feeling that the analytic situation has broken down. It is interesting to consider how it is that a therapy can be successfully maintained in the face of this unexpected interruption to the setting, and the loss of analytic anonymity, when consistency in both are so fundamental to the analytic method. An interruption to the basic analytic setting may often be an opportunity to consider one's theory of the analytic process itself.

Weiss (1975) concluded that the therapy is only really jeopardized by the failure to recognize the impact of the special event on the patient. In other words, external deviations, though not ideal, can be absorbed by the analytic process provided the therapist's capacity to function analytically is preserved, in the consistent attention paid to the patient's subjective inner world and in the consistent linking of external and internal realities. Ultimately, it is this "analytic function" which creates and maintains the "internal integrity of the analysis" as Fenster *et al.* (1986) aptly call it. According to this view, the patient's feeling of being accepted and cared for depends to a large extent on the therapist's interpretative function because his or her understanding of the patient is conveyed in what he or she selects for interpretation and especially in the *way* the interpretation is given:

> One may say that patients respond to our interpretations not only as tools which make them aware of the meaning of the unconscious and conscious processes, but also as reflections of the analyst's state of mind – particularly his ability to retain quietness and peacefulness and to focus on the central aspects of the patient's conscious and unconscious preoccupations and anxieties. The patient is also aware of the analyst's mind and memory through the way he holds together important external and internal factors and brings them together at the right time. [Rosenfeld, 1987, p. 31–32]

In the case of a "special event", this means acknowledging that something special and different has, in fact, occurred in external reality while continuing steadfastly to analyse its precise effect upon the patient's subjective internal reality as it is played out in the "total situation" of the transference.

In trying to understand this internal analytic function I find it helpful to distinguish analytic anonymity from analytic neutrality, although the two terms are often used interchangeably. Neutrality is variously described (and often used to refer to anonymity), but for the purposes of this discussion I am defining it as a dispassionate curiosity. It then emerges as an "ego-function" in its own right, and the essential component of a therapist's internal analytic function, giving rise to what Segal (1997) calls a "good counter-transference disposition". This is the basic disposition which allows a therapist to receive and emotionally identify with the patient's projections in her countertransference, whilst at the same time observing these feelings with curiosity, subjecting them to thought, and formulating a dispassionate interpretation about them. This internal function may go wrong, in principle, in one of two ways: the therapist may be unwilling to receive projections in the first place (in which case he or she will be experienced in the transference as an impenetrable "brick wall" sort of object who does not want to know what the patient is feeling); or the therapist may over-identify with what has been projected and not be able to think about it properly. It is this latter "deviation" from "normal counter-transference" (Money-Kyrle, 1956) which specifically disrupts analytic neutrality.

This is perhaps just a long way of saying that an analytic therapy is simply dependent upon the therapist's ability to keep analysing – with the proviso that "analysing" may need careful definition because it can mean different things for different people. However, the problem with many special events is that they do indeed interfere with the therapist's internal analytic function.

Pregnancy, for example, is a major developmental crisis in a woman's life (Raphael-Leff, 1980; 1986; 1993; Birkstead-Breen, 1986). Bibring (1959) has described it as a state of "benign depersonalisation" during which a process of "disintegration and reorganisation" is undertaken. Indeed, Birkstead-Breen (1986) argues that far from inducing a temporary state of disturbance from which the woman is eventually restored unchanged, the experience of pregnancy and birth offers her the opportunity to modify her internal object relationships in such a way that she will *not* be the same person as she was before. Essentially, she is working internally to achieve a new identity, as a mother, which means negotiating a new position in relation to her own internal mother, with all the attendant anxiety about usurping her place (Pines, 1972; 1982). Birkstead-Breen (1986) formulates this developmental task in terms of "how to become a woman with a baby rather than a girl with a doll". (An additional complication for the therapist is that she may be working to reconcile her sense of herself as both a professional woman and a mother, at least for her first pregnancy.) While so doing, a range of primitive anxieties are stirred up, for example about the state of the inside of her body, about losing identity or being annihilated, and about damaging or being damaged by the foetus, all of which need to be contained and worked through, often leaving the pregnant woman in a vulnerable state of emotional upheaval.

The taxing nature of this internal work certainly challenges the pregnant therapist's ability to hold onto her analytic function. In the earliest analytic paper on the pregnant therapist, Lax (1969) discusses a variety of countertransference difficulties, and describes the therapist's fearful or guilt-ridden anticipation of the patient's hostility or envy. Excessive concern or anger were especially evoked by the patient's sense of deprivation. I have indicated my own countertransference difficulties around informing patients of my pregnancy, though I found that returning to work (even part-time practice) with a small baby proved more difficult than working whilst pregnant. Quite apart from the practical difficulties of combining breastfeeding and sleepless nights with even part-time work, I found there to be a conflict between the demands of the real baby and those of the baby in the patient. To the extent that I fell back on an omnipotent wish to be the perfect ever-available mother to both baby and patient I was for a while more prone to react with impatience, stemming from guilt, when patients complained about being deprived by me. (In this respect, one will be most vulnerable to the guilt-inducing narcissistic or borderline patient who cannot tolerate the less-than-perfect mother.) Clementel-Jones (1985) refers to the "balancing act" required of the therapist who stands accused (or at any rate feels she does) of neglecting both the baby and the patient. Deben-Mager (1993) points out that a therapist will need to be very aware of her own "mothering needs" if the countertransference reaction of wanting to be the ideal mother is not to become too intense.

Denial may well be one response in this situation. The profound anxiety, rage and envy evoked by the pregnancy may feel too threatening for therapist as well as patient, and the therapist may seek to deny the significance of the intrusion. She may act as if nothing out of the ordinary has happened, or maintain a "business as usual" approach (Wedderkopp, 1990). There are many reports in the literature of a therapist finding herself reluctant to take up the issue and curiously blind to the patient's references to the pregnancy. In my case I could certainly feel the seductive pull of Miss A's "blissful" phantasy. It was tempting to free myself of guilt by joining her in it and going along with her idealization of my maternal qualities, rather than recognize the "harsh, cold" figure as a split-off aspect of me and seek to understand the anxieties leading her to take such refuge. Weiss (1975) refers to this, in different language, as the collusive wish of patient and therapist to return to the "safety and regression of the analytic situation and to the silent gratification of the transference" (p. 75).

An alternative response, and in a way the more potentially serious difficulty, is to acknowledge the altered circumstances but fail to respond in the normal analytic way to the intrusion, perhaps through loss of confidence in the analytic process. It is natural for the patient to try to deal with his or her anxiety about the intrusion (and apparent loss of containing function) by transforming the relationship into a more familiar sociable interaction. As Wedderkopp (1990) puts it: "There may occur solicitous enquiries about the therapist's health, her lifestyle, other children, as the patient began to mother the therapist-mother" (p. 41). The patient is projecting the child-in-need into the therapist, in order to get away from the intolerable feeling of being the motherless child-in-need. If, in turn, the therapist over-identifies with the projection, she may respond in kind (rather than analysing the patient's anxiety about the loss of the container), by becoming overly chatty, or self-revealing, or giving more information than is appropriate. Fenster et al. (1986) report that in a study (of twenty-two "psychoanalytically oriented psychotherapists") "participants judged themselves to be significantly more self-revealing than usual with their patients during the pregnancy. In addition, many of these therapists reported resisting the wish to be even more self-disclosing" (p. 54). Temporarily or otherwise, the therapist gives up analysing.

A therapist is more likely to over-identify with such projections and lose her analytic function if she is in a state of emotional or physical vulnerability. The ill analyst has a natural wish to be looked after, just as the patient is "offering" to do, and the pregnant therapist, perhaps for different reasons, may have a greater need to disclose than the patient has to hear the information. The danger is that the therapist's own need for gratification or closeness – which is natural in the circumstances, but misplaced – can interfere with her analytic function.

This enactment on the part of the therapist has interesting repercussions. The therapist may realize what is happening and recover her analytic function. Alternatively, she may seek to justify the lapse in her analytic function by rationalising it as a necessary alteration in technique (Langs, 1981). Lasky (1990), for example, comments that the understandable self-preoccupation of the ill analyst, and his or her "atypical readiness unconsciously to use the patient to obtain narcissistic gratifications" will interfere with the analyst's usual capacity to evaluate how much the patient needs to know about what is going on in the analyst's life. Referring to the analyst's wish to engage in a form of "narcissistic exhibitionism" he suggests that:

> Such a wish, when it remains unconscious (and therefore still narcissistic) can readily lead the analyst to a false conclusion that it is the patient's genuine need for information that has influenced his decision to be self-revealing. [p. 462]

In their discussion of technique, Fenster et al. (1986) rightly (in my view) point out that "virtually all communication from the patient must be seen as potentially reflective of the meaning of the pregnancy and the breach in the setting" (p. 49) but then state that "a change in focus" is necessary adequately to address the repercussions of the event. "The analyst's usual free-floating attention must give way to an alertness to the seemingly disparate disconnected associations, and implicit or explicit allusions to the pregnancy" (p. 50). In her anxiety to avoid denial and "curtail acting out", she recommends that the "pregnant therapist must actively pursue – through interpretations and questions – the significance and meaning of the pregnancy and the breach in the setting for the patient" (p. 51) and even that the pregnant therapist should make "cathartic interpretations" of unconscious material "without waiting for all the derivative material that ordinarily paves the way for an interpretation" (p. 52).

The question of whether or not altered circumstances necessitate a change in technique is a perennial one, but in my view most deviations in technique stem from a loss of confidence in the ordinary analytic process. I would argue that Fenster's recommended departure in technique, from normal free-floating attention to something much more active, is likely to be counter-therapeutic in its effect. Interpreting material too precipitately, before it is *possible* to know the full significance of the patient's communication, will simply make the patient suspect (correctly) that his or her therapist is too anxious. As Rosenfeld (1987) points out, in his discussion of therapeutic and anti-therapeutic factors in the therapist, the patient will not only experience this hasty interpretation as a rejection, but also as the therapist's defence against experiencing anxiety or uncertainty.

> There are many patients who are afraid to get into full contact with their deepest anxieties, so instead of feeling and knowing who and what they are, they pretend to know. If the analyst joins them in this activity, the therapeutic function of the analysis comes to a halt. [p. 37]

From this perspective, it is the therapist's capacity to maintain the *usual* degree of open-minded free-floating curiosity which is crucial, because it is only this non-anxious receptivity and thoughtfulness which allows the patient gradually to tolerate the anxiety provoked by his or her feelings and become able to hold them in mind.

Conclusion

Working analytically through a pregnancy can be profoundly enriching, for both patient and therapist, and I think there may be two reasons for this. Alongside all the anger and envy there is usually some sense of relief in the obvious creativity of the therapist, a welcome sign, perhaps, that she is not as damaged as the patient had feared. The pregnant woman is, after all, the most potent reparative symbol of continuing and future life. But perhaps the chief relief, for patient and therapist, comes from the therapist's ability to maintain her analytic function. Thus does she really show the patient that her mind is intact and functioning, in difficult circumstances, and thus does her confidence in the analytic process deepen.

CHAPTER SIX

The crouching monk: disability in the consulting room

Marie Conyers

Introduction

W hen I was invited to contribute a chapter to this volume on the theme of difference my immediate response was an amalgam of feelings. I was flattered, anxious that my paper would not be good enough, and intrigued, but I also had a sense of wry amusement because "difference" has been an ever-present theme in my consulting room. What seems self-evident, but

I feel also needs to be stated, is that in all consulting rooms there will be differences that come to bear on the work.

I am registered as partially sighted and people notice that my pupils are elongated, giving my eyes a somewhat catlike appearance. Due to congenital cerebral palsy, I also formerly walked with a limp which was recently corrected through surgical intervention. The operation meant I took a six-week break from work, after which I used crutches, not knowing at the time how long it would be before I would be able to walk unaided.

This chapter aims to examine the significance for my patients and myself of the impact of my new disability, and will hopefully stimulate others into further thought about the impact of physical differences, temporary and permanent, in the consulting room.

Psychotherapy and disability

Throughout my work I have been watchful and reflective about the timing and the inner-world significance when patients consciously or unconsciously allude to my disability. I aim to note the impact of such allusions on the transference, and I also note my counter-transference resonance. When disability feels "alive" in the material I encourage patients to expand and make connections, and I make interpretations of this material as and when I feel it to be appropriate. However, there has been a surprising dearth of reaction to my disability from my able-bodied patients, although where there has been a reaction it has been swift and powerful.

On one occasion in an assessment session, a female patient needed to know very early on whether I could see her clearly. I responded gently that I could see her very clearly, and I went on to comment that it might be of importance for her, perhaps on many levels, to be seen clearly. I was aware of the anger in her voice as she made the enquiry and I speculated that vision, or lack of it, might have a significance in her internal world. The patient had disclosed that her mother was diagnosed with a neurological condition and, both symbolically and physically, had been unable to see her for a very long time. The understanding from this material formed the basis for my decision to answer her question unequivocally, as I felt to withhold might increase her anxieties and fantasies to an unbearable level, particularly at such an embryonic stage in the work. Despite my addressing what it might mean for this patient to be seen, she decided not to commence therapy with me on the basis that she could not cope with my disability. Perhaps her hope that her inner needs might be clearly held and witnessed was overpowered by her fear that this would not be possible with an impaired mother/therapist. She may also have felt unconscious terror at the prospect of her needs being held and witnessed by me.

On another occasion, a patient informed me in his second visit that I was the most hideous, repulsive person he had ever seen. Whilst this was difficult and painful to hear, I utilized what Casement (1985) would call the internal supervisor to understand that his attack was an expression of his terror. It was also an unconscious test to establish whether I was strong enough to contain him. On this occasion our work did continue for many years, though interestingly it wasn't until he had been in therapy for some months that he noticed with a jolt of surprise that I *did* have a couch in my consulting room. I believe this was his metaphor for giving me professional validity. It was as if he could only then see clearly that I was a bona fide therapist who could provide him with something useful.

At this stage in the process, when a greater level of trust had been established, I ventured that perhaps he'd wanted me to react to his earlier attack – his seeing me as hideous – because he had always struggled with self-image and others' superficial assessments of him. To know that something painful and hideous could be managed and heard without retaliation perhaps ultimately led him to a place where he could take something useful from the therapy.

With patients who have physical problems or who are in the process of becoming disabled through some form of degenerative illness, my difference is more present in the therapy and appears to have subtle and varied meanings. There is less repression and generally speaking my impairment is alluded to earlier on in the therapeutic process, and is variously fantasized that "I will more readily understand where they are coming from" or that my professional achievement gives them hope to transcend their impairment, a sense of "anything is possible". I am also watchful for possible envy of what I have achieved (an imagined status in their minds) which they might feel eludes them.

The impact of my absence and return on crutches

During April 2003 I had to undergo a planned total knee replacement and I had been advised that when I returned to work after six weeks I would be on crutches and sticks for many months to come. In discussion with a colleague we agreed that whether or not an explanation was given for this unusual six-week break there would be an impact. Material would emerge either way and would have to be worked through. On balance, it felt to me that the human, ethical and courteous option was to give patients the briefest explanation, and I decided to inform them that I had to have surgery and would be away for six weeks.

It could be argued that becoming crutch-bound as a result of a surgical intervention provided a powerful metaphor for the psychotherapeutic process. In my case an operation/intervention to put right a congenital defect led to greater, temporary disability. In psychotherapy, patients commonly report feeling worse before they feel better and it is useful to think in terms of time for rehabilitation, and the need to be patient while the healing process takes its course.

Terror, rage, survival and "warts an' all" rehabilitation

I will now draw on material from four of my patients to illustrate the impact of my using crutches and the emotional grist this threw up for our work.

Teresa

In the first session following my return to work an apparent unconscious synchronicity occurred between myself and Teresa, an ebullient, warm, increasingly emotionally aware patient who had attended therapy once weekly for some three years. The session started with Teresa commenting on my crutches. Two minutes into the session the telephone in my consulting room, normally turned off but inadvertently left on after the six-week break, rang shrilly. I retrieved my crutches and, apologizing, walked across the room to switch off the phone. Teresa commented that it was just amazing to see how different I was. I wondered with her about this idea of difference. Teresa said she had so much to tell me – something had shifted. However, she looked puzzled, stating that during the break she had resumed taking one Seroxat "to keep her on an even keel". Until this time she had been steadily decreasing her medication.

Teresa then talked at length about how furious she felt with her father-in-law who had just undergone a knee replacement. She was vehemently expressive of the despair and annoyance she felt with her father-in-law who she perceived as being dependent on others to take care of his every whim. She described him as resplendent in his incapability, sitting there, obese and huge, over-reliant on an unnecessary wheelchair, everyone making a fuss. My patient feared her father-in-law would voraciously feed on ever-increasing attention. Teresa began to realize that within that family unit she could no longer collude with this stance and she spoke in disgust about her father-in-law's first post-operative outing. As I wondered about the transferential reference in this our first session following my post-operative return to work, Teresa related that everyone danced in attendance on the invalid who then vomited up his dinner on the table. Teresa had no conscious way of knowing of course that I'd had a knee replacement, but her rage had clearly been displaced onto her father-in-law who became the useless object. I wondered with her about the possible unconscious displacement of her fury at me onto her father-in-law and her possible desire to vomit out this session. She was able to reflect on this and acknowledge the truth in it.

Furthermore, I internally mused on Teresa's enormous envy of her father-in-law's ability to allow himself to be dependent, ask for help and be cared for. I was reminded of earlier material – as a child Teresa had been run over. She'd never told her mother about the accident when she'd gone home, making herself invisible and invincible as a defence against the feeling that mother wouldn't care anyway. The paradox for this defensively humorous, affable, self-care-taking lady was the infinite longing and unexpressed envy that someone else could so blatantly need and demand. Perhaps her terror was that I might be too needy myself and therefore want something from her or at the very least not be strong enough to hold her. The crutch itself has so many archetypal and historical resonances, bringing up images of the helpless cripple, someone who cannot stand unaided. Teresa's unconscious terror seemed to be that

I would be unable to hold her in my mind and be too needy myself to see her pain and internal injury.

I then spoke to Teresa's desire to become dependent and her terror that I would not be emotionally available. Hence, it was as if she had to comfort and contain herself orally by the ingestion of anti-depressants as a defence against a potentially withholding breast (Klein, 1988).

Teresa, I believe, had suffered from primary maternal failure. Her mother was absent a lot in the first year of her life and from Teresa's account never answered her cries as a toddler, derisively nicknaming her as "a cry baby drama queen". Thus at the time of her greatest need when she had been in a car accident she did not believe that her physical frailty and emotional needs would be appropriately met by her mother (Winnicott, 1988a).

Later in the session Teresa laughingly imagined that I had had a knee replacement and that I would know how rehabilitation should proceed. I thought this rehabilitated me in her mind as someone who could make "the right recovery"; that therapy with me might embody for her, and me, a projection of hope for the possibility of emergence from dependence on symbolic crutches, i.e. the therapeutic process, towards independence and symbolic emotional mobility in Teresa's outer adult world, an unconscious longing for wholeness.

Jane

During the session following the break in therapy for my operation, another patient, Jane, raised concern about whether her baby grandson was fed well enough. I wondered about the multi-layered meaning of this statement. Jane reported feeling immobilized in relation to both her grandson and her daughter as she did not want to be seen as interfering, overbearing and dominant. She feared repeating the punitive relationship she experienced with her own mother both as a child and as a woman. However, she was intermittently enraged and extremely tearful about her own paralysis. She was in touch with the child within her, not knowing what to do "as if hiding under the table".

Countertransferentially I held and wondered about this on several levels. Did she feel she was getting a good enough feed here? Or did she feel she had been left crying in the break with the "food" of therapy tantalizingly out of reach? Jane's gradual ability to survive the disappointment of my humanity was being put to the test. Her fantasy "demand" that I must be "perfect" was called into question both through the need for surgery and through my absence, which maternally failed her, as in her childhood when Jane had been left wanting on so many levels.

Breaks in the therapy had always been emotionally agonizing for Jane, and I interpreted to her that she needed to know that I did see her distress and that she may have felt that she was left with too little to survive on during the break. Jane characteristically nodded, making no comment. Then, at the end of this first session, instead of saying "See you on Wednesday", I said "See you next week" and I saw the look of absolute rage cross Jane's face and, inwardly shocked at my error, in an unprocessed reaction, I began to hastily apologize, saying I had got temporarily muddled.

I was internally irritated at my own mishandling but simultaneously intrigued about why I had somehow got hooked into a muddled confusion with this patient. Muddled confusion was a recurring theme for Jane, frequently struggling to find the right words, half finished sentences, self-corrections, smacking her knees, talking about muddle.

At the next session Jane began to tell me how she was dreading seeing her ophthalmologist for her six-month review (for eye laser treatment). Jane felt she wouldn't normally have picked such an ophthalmologist whom she saw as overbearing, confident, upright and extremely tall. This consultant exuded power in every stride of her body. Jane gave examples of two other doctors who had misdiagnosed her condition, but this (idealized) consultant had it "spot on, perfect, right". Her analogy of the consultant's perfection and uprightness juxtaposed with my confusion of the days was an obvious attack on my error and had to be responded to. I ventured that I was hearing that she was extremely angry at my mistake at the end of the last session, for which I apologized again. Jane then said that it was not good enough, and she would not hear apologies, or accept any middle-road notion of good enough. Therapists had no business to make mistakes, they had to be perfect. Jane felt I had let her down badly and not for the first time. Jane continued that she could not now hold me in mind as anything. In her imagination I would not be there as a supporting influence while she went through the ordeal in the hospital. Intra-psychically I had been completely split off from the internal good object of the earlier days of our work. I decided to stay silent (guiltily berating myself, agreeing that I *had* let her down) but feeling that anything I might say would only add fuel to an already stoked fire for my patient.

Engaging with my "internal supervisor" I was able to consider the notion of this mistake demonstrating our capacity and fallibility to be drawn unconsciously into our patients' internal muddle. I had not wanted to collude with Jane's idealization – perhaps unconsciously I had made a mistake in order to emphasize my falli-bility, and yet in my engagement with my own super-ego I was perhaps struggling with my disappointment at my fallibility. Thus I had become the criticized child and she the powerfully enraged mother, something which to her and possibly to me at this point felt terrifyingly un-survivable.

I have come to see that, at a point where neither of us could see clearly, Jane's murderous rage had succeeded in knocking me off my "therapeutic crutches". Jane was caught and struggling with the idea of a link between sight, uprightness and perfection. She was grappling with how to manage to accept that the perfect yet daunting ophthalmologist was unsatisfactory, and that the imperfect ophthalmologist, the wounded healer, might be good enough.

The positive symbol in my being physically marred, but still able to stay with her rage and pain in subsequent sessions, was some-thing that she had been unable to test out in her overwhelmed state with the ophthalmologist. Here the transference was split. The ophthalmologist she was both afraid and in awe of, was reminiscent of a powerfully striding mother. In having to witness my physical dependence on crutches, having just survived being alone in the break and then being met with the ill-timed mistake on my return, lay the seed for the paradoxical struggle to appreciate that vulner-ability and imperfection can potentially facilitate strength and development. In relation to the ophthalmologist Jane was paralyzed through fear that she would have to hold on to and own all her neediness, weakness and vulnerability.

I mused that I had become the unconscious conduit to test out either the limits of masochistic endurance, i.e. in the bearing of the mistake, but possibly also the struggle for the survival of it. That Jane could carry on working with me when I was so obviously less than perfect and stay with her fury, working it through rather than rejecting her therapy in the way that she had felt previously rejected by her earlier therapist, was, I think, an important emotional benchmark.

Jane's terror and awareness of madness represented by her mother and re-enforced by the tragic suicide of her partner was traumatically painful and Jane had been let down at so many very important stages of her life and had had no satisfactory ending with her partner. In her rage and fury that I had unconsciously got into a "mad muddle" depriving her of her second session in the week, thereby symbolically depriving her of my presence, Jane must have felt that I had become like her mother and that I was throwing her out just like her (perceived) experience of her former therapist.

The session following my return to work reminded me of periods where Jane would oscillate between taunting and attacking me as useless, projecting unbearable feelings of inadequacy onto me in an attempt to test out the limits of my and our endurance.

Jane's ability to allow containment in the face of the disappointment of seeing me crutch-bound, symbolically marred, was evidence of a significant shift in her internal world. Jane has begun to show an increasing ability to empathize and be aware of the needs of her young grandson, and to display tenderness where previously everything had been marked with "not my business", "nothing to do with me". All her earlier defences against feelings and attachments are apparently lessening. Jane feels she is "more real" and different. She comments that she is aware of her need to "talk to me in fantasy" when in moments of indecision and uncertainty. I am also held in mind as a person of inner peace and calm. I am reminded of Hobson when he writes: "The 'heartbeat' of therapy is a process of learning how to go on becoming a person together with others. That learning never ends" (Hobson, 1985, p. xii).

At the time of writing I am no longer on crutches or sticks. I have been intrigued that Jane has made no conscious reference to this change. It may be enough that I have been able to move from being on crutches to standing unaided again. And we have both survived the break, the intrusiveness of my surgery, my incapacitation and my imperfection. Whether Jane's anger might have gone

underground again or be waiting for another opportunity of expression remains to be seen. For Jane to arrive at and to stay in the
middle ground of not knowing and to sense the notion of "good
enough holding" as a releasing potential, is something which was
unconsciously activated throughout the term of her therapy and
which was perhaps most consciously crystallized at the particular
juncture of my return to work on crutches.

Ian

Eight weeks following the resumption of therapy after the break, I
transferred from crutches to two sticks (a metaphoric halfway
house). Another patient, Ian, commented on my sticks, the change,
and said perhaps we were both "getting there". I wondered where in
his inner world "there" might be. Ian continued to muse on the
rightness of his decision to give up work, to have a space and not to
over-analyze.

I speculated on his terror of getting somewhere difficult and painful. Ian began to cry in the silence, shaking, saying he was touching
something deep, something painful, something real within. He felt
there was no need for words here and sensed that I understood. I
wondered to myself about idealization as a defence against negative
transference, the notion of an intrusive fantasy that I could see into
him, read his mind, understand him without words; the longing for
a magical fit. I thought of the joy that such a fantasy might give rise
to, i.e. the intimacy of being known in one's inner world in the face
of feeling utterly alone. The main theme of our work thus far had
been Ian's sorrow and grief at having to give up an intense love
affair and sustain a marriage where he still loved his partner. Ian had
frequently spoken of a deep sense of inner loneliness with links
to the death of his beloved mother. I found myself thinking about
the ultimate realization that one had to face one's own human
aloneness.

It may be that Ian's denial of separateness was shown in his
combining us in the comment about "getting there". My difference
was used to serve his defensive need to fantasise that I had some
sort of archetypal second or special sight which allowed me to
magically know what he was feeling and thus there would be no
need for him to talk. I was reminded of the blind seer in ancient

mythology and culture and of "the loneliness that lies at the heart of psychotherapy and indeed of all personal relationships" (Hobson, 1985, p. xv).

Because of the unusually timed prolonged break in therapy I spoke about Ian seeing me as another abandoning soulmate, and how his defensive substitution – the idealization that I would "know without words" – was perhaps a way of protecting both himself and myself from his rage at my not having been there.

Crutches are a powerful symbol. How can patients consciously, rationally express anger when they are caught up in a society which suggests we must be "sympathetic/understanding/accepting" of disability? As Ian took particular pride in being a right-thinking sort of person I think he needed to believe I could "see" the rage within him without him needing to express it in words, and that this would be understandable and all right.

I spoke about his courage to struggle and stay in this space, and wondered about the conflict in him between his longing for intimacy, his fear of his unconscious rage and his sense of abandonment and isolation in the break. Through his tears Ian said that it was as if I had, out of a mist of his pain, made sense of something for him. Only then did he begin to talk about his ambivalence; wanting to take flight, to give up therapy, in his disappointment that analyzing didn't take away the pain of his losses, set against his longing to carry on and his sense of being held here, the only place where he could allow what at times felt like overwhelming sadness and depression.

Finally I present some work with a patient whom I shall call Susan, who provided me with the title for this chapter.

Susan

Susan was working towards a planned ending after five years of once-weekly psychotherapy and was wondering how she was going to manage, how she would cope with the mixed emotions of the hope, the fear and the uncertainty of what life without the therapeutic space would mean. It was important that she had made the decision about when to end her therapy because her first experience of therapy had ended very badly. As part of a training requirement she had been forced to move from an unregistered psychotherapist and start work with me. This had many resonances with primitive fears and experiences, which we had worked through during the years of our time together, and consequently Susan was now feeling more in control of her life and more her own person.

Much of the material centred on Susan's retirement in the next year; in addition to giving up her symbolic family, her colleagues, she also had to deal with the possibility of abdominal surgery. Was I the unconscious symbol of survival from surgery? We had previously considered in detail the losses and implications for her of having such a procedure. Susan mused on the notion of having increased time for herself, i.e. as much sick leave as required. She spoke of coming to realize through this process that her mother wouldn't change, that she'd given what she could and that had to be accepted and used for what is was. Retrospectively I realize that this could have been anxiety about the gift she was to give me and any possible interpretations I might make of this.

I wondered about the resonances here. She spoke of needing the affirmation and praise of others and I transferentially interpreted that it was as if she wanted me to send her out into the world with my blessings. Susan had struggled for adult separation from perceived cloying parents, particularly surrounding maternal separation and ambivalent attachment. After some thought Susan continued that she felt she had always had "blessing" here even from the beginning when she wouldn't admit it to herself and was so angry.

After a pause she said she had a gift for me, would I accept it? I wondered what this gift might mean and decided to explore it with her. I have always debated this controversial aspect of our work and recognize that each scenario with each particular patient has to be responded to uniquely, borne out from the experience of our work with each patient, their history, transference and countertransference responses.

In Susan's case I felt that it might be perceived as extremely rejecting to refuse a small token gift. So I nodded, and she gave me a small cast of a curled-up crouching monk. Susan said she'd bought it because she had thought of me "and this crouching monk could leap to his feet and jump up". Internally I noted the reference to my "crouchedness" and her longing to know that I would leap up and survive, would walk again without sticks, and at the same time I wondered about her sadistic attack hidden in the loving gift.

However, I merely intimated that the monk also looked mischievous and I wondered where that really lay. Susan laughed and said mainly in her, but she also felt she detected a mischievous twinkle in my eye sometimes and that was something she liked. The card she gave read, "Love is the space that lets us be who we really are". I thanked her for her present and chose to explore with her the possible symbolism. I noted that the monk was something carved out of the past (a reproduction of a medieval misericord). Symbolically, the medieval period, that age, had now gone, was in the past. The gift was now complete, a rounded object and it was potentially something precious for her as a metaphor. From crouching and being small, feeling insignificant throughout a lot of her life, she could perhaps also stand out, or in her words "leap up". However, at the same time, I was in no doubt that this interpretation was salient and applicable to both of us, as so often in the dialectic flow between patient and therapist.

Conclusion

This chapter has attempted an exploration of the alchemy that existed between my patients and myself created by the difference I brought into the consulting room by walking on crutches and then moving to sticks. I have shown that reactions ranged from feelings of terror, rage and anxieties about, and hope for, survival, to thoughts about rehabilitation. I have noted the enormity of the rage associated with the terror that the wounded healer might not be able to see clearly, nor adequately contain her patients, and the difficulty patients have in directing this rage at someone who is disabled. Hence much of it was projected onto others in the first instance. I have also noted the deep sadness that awareness of life's limitations brings, and how my disability and gradual recovery was seen as a metaphor of potential unconscious hope about survival "warts an' all", because at some level we are all disabled, some more obviously than others.

Through the presentation of the crouching monk, Susan had encapsulated this reality in a way that other patients could not always articulate. They all saw me as more fragile on my crutches and yet I was still able, hopefully, to contain them sufficiently. That a therapist can be impaired and still function, be damaged yet of value does, I think, contain the potential for hope within psychotherapy.

When I was finally able to walk without any assistance, and was walking better than I had done through most of my life, one patient merely commented, "you are better". The fantasy that underlies the statement that one can go from crutches one week to being better or indeed completely cured is part of the deepest longing that all patients bring into therapy, together with the hope that the therapist has the formula that will bring about this longed-for state of affairs. In holding the meanings, possibilities and realities, both conscious and unconscious, that mark the uniqueness and complexity of our work, my patients and I had to stay with, and come through, the physical changes and their symbolic resonance in our inner worlds. The quiet waiting and seeing what might evolve, the outcome that might emerge, the hesitant steps that become possible, are all a powerful analogy for the work of psychotherapy.

Ultimately, perhaps ironically, the "differences" between my patients and myself were not so great. I too had to stay with the terror of how my "new self" in her altered appearance would be perceived and responded to, as well as holding on to the hope for a rehabilitation that would lead me to a better place. Thus perhaps the crouching monk and I are not so far apart, and serve as symbols of both terror and hope. With time, all things move on; there is always change and there is always difference.

CHAPTER SEVEN

Paying for love in the helping professions: contradictions inherent in charging fees for psychotherapy

Steven Mendoza

There are those who assume that there *are* inherent contradictions in charging fees for psychotherapy and there are those would not hold any contradictions to be inherent in charging fees. I think of those for whom inherent contradictions *are* implicit as those for whom charging is inconsistent with the aspect of loving. I think that loving here means acting to benefit others from the motivation of a state of mind enjoying the blissful enhancement of emotion and thought which comes from knowing that one is doing good. Paradoxically, of course, the process of psychotherapy may entail, for the psychotherapist, feelings which are anything but beatific, such as inadequacy, impotence, frustration, rage, shame and guilt. Better, then, we should be paid for such love in some other coin than a toll of gratitude that would block the very psychotherapy it paid for. Hence Winnicott's (1947) formulation, not of love but of hate, as restricted in the countertransference to the two prerogatives of charging for sessions and of ending them on time.

Perhaps it is because I worked for a local authority as a social worker that I think of those of us for whom these contradictions are implicitly inherent as wedded to the ethos of public service and probably to the ethos of socialism too. We feel that human needs should be met out of compassion by the individual and by society. Saint Paul called this spirit charity but that word has changed in meaning now from caritas, or care, to conscience money. As we think about paying for love it might be helpful to recall that the politically correct understanding of charity and pity is no longer care and compassionate piety but is now the belittling of a recipient by the attribution to him of emotional needs. If they have become these, what has love become and what kind of love is it we pay for?

The ethos of public service and the individual motive of compassion rather than the motive *to* remuneration are worthy and these are excellent principles. Those who have a public service post and those who are content to live within what means they have so as to succour clients for free are in these respects virtuous. But there is a spirit which goes farther than this enjoyment of personal merit, saying that those who do not work from either of these principles but who charge are greedy and unscrupulous, not part of the solution, and therefore part of the problem, objects of moral condemnation and political harangue. It is a familiar contradiction that a worthy disposition of social responsibility and personal charity has become a disposition of persecutory indignation and of moral outrage which may actually be false morality in the particular meaning "without-ness" that Bion (1962c) gives the term:

> It is an envious assertion of moral superiority without any morals. In short it is the resultant of an envious stripping or denudation of all good . . . The process of denudation continues till $- \male - \female$ represent hardly more than an empty superiority-inferiority that in turn degenerates to nullity. (Bion, 1962, p. 97)

Whenever we set our own goodness not in relation to a spiritual ideal but in contrast to the badness of another it behoves members of our professions particularly to consider the possibility that some projective mechanism is at work.

But if we can be quick to condemn those we think are making more money than we do then some of our patients too have their own way of relating to these principles. Some report the feeling of resentment at paying not because they think the psychotherapist is greedy, although they may do, but because they attribute their disturbance, often with validity, to the failures of their parents. They describe quite sympathetically their resentment at paying to amend damage for which others are responsible. To get better is to let the parents off. Here I think conflicts about paying may have clinical significance. But it is the getting better which lets off the miscreant parents more than the paying. While fees may be the first indication it is this which is the clinical issue: that to agree to enjoy life and to see things the way they are we have to mourn for the lost chance of visiting upon parents the sadistic reprisals they "deserve". Progress in psychotherapy may depend upon arriving at a confidence in the object which allows the patient to forgo the addictive certainty of fantasies of retaliation. Instead we have to settle for the uncertainties of love coming, as it does, from autonomous people. No wonder, then, that some patients, to their chagrin, feel they can get love, and usually not even that, only by paying a psychotherapist.

I suggest that many of us have within us the stereotype of the greedy analyst. Naturally he lives in Hampstead, naturally he is a man, naturally he practises in Harley Street and of course he charges astronomical fees, seeing only those who can afford them. Many of those, of course, have money but no sense and have been manipulated by this creature into a lifelong dependency, never getting better and, inconsistently, not having anything wrong with them. It is not that there are no unscrupulous, fashionable practitioners. It *is* that the stereotype of the greedy analyst is an inner object, sometimes an object of self-righteous persecution which denies its own guilt and sometimes one of plain envy.

In social anthropology both the virtue of public service and the professional who subsists upon his earnings are found. The shamans of the near Arctic who are so fascinatingly described by Eliade (1982), particularly through the field work of Rasmussen, do not charge for their work of divination and healing. They tend to be the dominant personalities in their groups, the best hunters, the most wily and powerful. To be a shaman is their destiny. The prospective shaman contracts in early adulthood a life threatening disease whose only remedy is to be a shaman. The local shaman takes him away and hangs him, like Odin, in a tree or subjects him to other ordeals leading to experiences of trance and contact with animal spirit guides and other spirits. He learns to divine the location of game and the vagaries of the weather. He learns to follow the trail of the lost soul to the hideout of the appropriating spirit and by trickery or main force he retrieves it. These are powerful and charismatic men. This shaman is probably as much an inner object as the greedy analyst. The point is that he is self-sufficient, not depending on his art to live but living off the country like his companions. Perhaps a living is easier to get in the near Arctic.

With this character we can contrast one that could be called the witch doctor. He lives ostentatiously, requiring expensive consignments of cloth and other goods for his services. In Beattie and Middleton's (1969) book on spirit possession the expense of the dispossession ritual is presented as part of the healing process. The possessing spirits are remarkable for their contemporaneity. Thus in a recently discovered tribe there sometimes was a vogue for possession by the aeroplane spirit. The afflicted woman, for the patient is often female, has to learn an elaborate dance for which the participation of many other group members is required. Naturally it has to be made worth their while in food and drink. For some husbands then, there is the implication that attending your wife properly may be good insurance against her getting depressed and having some spirit move in on her, an expensive business. The equivalent obtains in the west: the rich man's wife and her expensive analysis, or indeed her peccadillo with the tennis coach. And what it is that a husband resorts to when it is he who feels neglected?

The difficulties addressed in psychotherapy do have their social and family context as well as their dynamics in analysis. Treatment itself is a social institution and may, including issues of payment, be the more effective psychotherapy for consideration of such matters. The shaman appears better in this account than the witch doctor.

To conclude this excursion there is a telling story, from Eliade (1982) again, of the degenerate shamans who secrete a lint of cotton in their mouths and, biting their cheeks suffuse it with blood. They suck on the patient and produce the bloody lint showing that they have sucked out the bloody worm of the illness. The story so far is a disparaging attack on the psychotherapist as a charlatan. The point is that these shamans believe that the shamans up the river, presumably in less sophisticated climes, really do suck out the bloody worm.

Similarly, in the consulting room, when I cannot understand what is going on, I may feel that a proper psychotherapist would have a metapsychologically sophisticated, clear and true understanding of the process. But patients do sometimes need to find in us feelings of inauthenticity. Also we may feel unhappy about charging if we have not analyzed properly the feeling that we give nothing of value. Of course the denial can always take the manic form of a greedy insistence on the inflated value of our work and the refusal to be self-critical.

As a last anthropological topic there are the gift economies of the Pacific North West of America and the Trobriand Islanders of the Pacific archipelagos, perhaps even Polynesia itself. In British Columbia, the Pacific North West, the process in question is called the Potlach: social occasions require one man to make gifts to another. The more goods he imposes upon him the greater the triumph of his superior economic potency, and the more dismay his rival feels at the prospect of having to exceed this bounty, capable of sinking the vessel it invests. Thus an ever-growing pile of blankets may do the rounds of far-flung settlements. The process might be seen as institutionalizing the impulse to triumph so as to depotentiate it. Konrad Lorenz (1963) in his book *On Aggression*, described displays enabling animals to save themselves the expense of actual fighting. Football serves, without complete success, to contain the impulse to internecine war.

But there are psychodynamic limits to what might appear to be virtue in political systems and social norms. The virtue of generosity is limited by the psychodynamics of triumph. And for a psychoanalytic practitioner, of course, triumph is always, finally, an Oedipal and narcissistic triumph over our infantile dependency.

This is no place to arbitrate among the respective proprieties of public and private services. But some comments on work in the Health Service and in charities may be relevant. A patient referred by Mind in the early 1980s was angry to discover that, in addition to the fee he paid me from his benefits, I had a small subsidy for each session, paid by Mind. I never learned what it was about this which incensed him. I think it may have been simply that he was not told. It may have been that he, resenting paying out of so small a disposable income, felt that I did not need his fee when I was paid by the charity.

His status as the patient of an institution had other consequences as well as matters of payment: without consulting me the head of the branch of Mind intervened with the patient's psychiatrist to have his medication discontinued. At that time Mind felt that medication was an act of violence against the patient. As a result of this his schizophrenia, supposed at the time to be a social artefact, reasserted itself, leading him to take off his trousers and set a small fire in the courtyard of the Mind office premises. For him this was not funny and led to his detention in a large mental hospital under a court order. His psychotherapy with me was interrupted for some months and when he returned, not having informed me of his detention, I charged him, at the behest of the head, for the missed sessions.

Today, being more independent, I might not have charged him for such an involuntary dereliction. It seems to me that the ethos of the organization at the time adhered unthinkingly, even autistically, to received ideas of propriety in psychiatry and with equal adhesiveness to the principles of psychoanalytic practice as edicts to be applied without respect to the circumstances of the individual. Here too we can see the dangers of political correctness when it is used as a substitute for thought, and of institutional intervention between what should be a bounded dyad.

There may be other drawbacks to the institutional care of patients in a psychoanalytic, or, at worst, a pseudo-psychoanalytic setting. Patients may find themselves offered treatments whose length is determined not by clinical needs but by budgets which share the supposed benefits of analytic treatments thinly among a large population. Such patients may wait a couple of years for six months of once-weekly sessions. Those who are more familiar than I am with such work may be able to judge whether the provision is worth the patient's while and whether it makes proper clinical application of the style of psychotherapy. Another style of treatment might be more appropriate to such a limited provision.

Limits of resources impose a rather arbitrary provision with respect to individual needs. This in its turn imposes a technical problem: the public health patient in analytical work is the passive subject of allocation, not the active party to a contract. He or she is in a state of actual dependence. This must be contrasted to the transferential, as against actual, dependence in the transference. The whole point of psychoanalysis is to establish contact with infantile parts of the self and to find in the inner world a container for those parts. This is an interplay between adult and infantile parts of the self. We need, and hope to acquire through analysis, a dual sense of our vulnerable, undeveloped states of mind and a sense of something protective and containing in us which makes dependency bearable. Such is the severity of the challenge to bear dependency that Scott Peck's (1978) famous book, *The Road Less Travelled* actually proscribes any emotional need of a partner, prescribing only selfless, independent, love as a basis for marriage. This principle is repeated in many schools of psychotherapy and infantile neediness is, perhaps, as unacceptable an aspect of psychoanalysis, to many, as envy and infantile destructiveness. Usually psychoanalysis has the adult contract with the patient to contrast with the regression in the transference. When the patient is a recipient of state provision and therefore actually dependent this has to be taken into account in the analysis.

It might be said that the patient who receives free treatment is infantilized by that and, in the same vein of possible rationalization, that the patient who pays retains his adult status as a client of the psychotherapist, who then has a reciprocal dependency directly on his patient. This is interesting because of the subtlety of the nature of regression in psychoanalysis. It seems to me that this is one good function of the tradition in the Institute of Psychoanalysis of addressing the patient as Mr or Mrs, for this emphasizes the adult status of the patient within which he has therapeutic experiences of infantile states of mind.

To have the help of a psychoanalyst to bear the helplessness of our need for help and the devastating emotions of apprehending the beauty of someone who understands and cares for us may be very different from an actual regression which may have an abreactive quality. Paying, as an adult, for the privilege of accommodating our neediness, may protect against abreaction and foster ego-relatedness even to our own infantile components. Of course such a privilege is available only to those who have the means. What could never be promulgated would be the principle that only by paying could such an accommodation be made. Patients who have to receive free or nominally charged treatment do not seem to me to suffer from any serious drawback to the efficacy of their treatment. Such a reservation must limit the significance of what I suggest. In practice I think the situation is covered adequately by the reservation that principles are not applied arbitrarily but according to the circumstances obtaining at the time. In other words, if you can pay, then that is your good fortune and you should. If you cannot pay, then, as I will discuss, you may feel that you have to pay in gratitude and this may need to be analyzed.

As for the psychotherapist's dynamics attending being paid, I have mentioned his feeling that he does not deserve it and his feeling that he deserves too much. Perhaps his sense of financial dependency on the patient keeps him in mind of the equality which every human being has with every other.

The client who does pay is not paying for love. The greatest fortune that can fall to a student of Buddhism is to give the Dharma, literally, truth, the wisdom in which Buddhism insists, and which provides the means to the cessation of suffering, to another suffering person, the assumption being that all sentient beings who have not yet attained enlightenment do, whether they can understand it or not, suffer. It is taught that only the kindness of the Buddha, like the kindness of the mother herself, can show us this path. It is this love, realized as wisdom, which makes salvation possible.

Here, perhaps, is a good expression of our sense that there is an inherent contradiction in charging for our work. Buddhist teachings are never charged for, nor is a teacher of Dharma ever paid. But for his subsistence offerings may be made and, indeed, a student requesting teachings would see his act of generosity in making such an offering as conferring upon him the benefits to his practice of accumulating essential merit. Of course any expression of generosity will do, and the recipient does not have to be a Buddhist. An ordained teacher will almost certainly receive something, but a lay teacher, having his own livelihood, equally is *un*likely to need, and therefore to receive, any honorarium. My wife and colleague, Mrs Patricia Mendoza, points out that, similarly, a psychotherapist may charge for his or her necessary expenses of living, for his time but not for his love. Love is not a faculty that can be deployed at will. Love is evoked by the object, not at the behest of either party. But the faculty of love is essential to good practice. In psychoanalytic work love involves the analysis of countertransference hate, and the goal of analysis is the tolerance of ambivalence. The practitioner must do this if the patient is to do it. When we select trainees we never specify love as a criterion but always we require the capacity to realize an analytic state of mind.

I remember the late Chad Vara addressing a student audience on the subject of depression in 1964 and saying that the patient pays for the privilege of being hostile to the psychotherapist. He might have added that the patient also pays to assuage his guilt. If he does not pay then the treatment must consider how the patient's hate and the failure of love *are* contained. Obviously, if they are contained by paying then this must be analyzed too.

Klein (1957 [1977]) treats of gratitude in her ultimate paper "Envy and Gratitude" saying:

> One major derivative of the capacity for love is the feeling of gratitude. Gratitude is essential in building up the relation to the good object and underlies also the appreciation of goodness in others and in oneself. Gratitude is rooted in the emotions and attitudes that arise in the earliest stage of infancy, when for the baby the mother is the one and only object. I have referred to this early bond[1] as the basis for all later relations with one loved person. While the exclusive relation to the mother varies individually in duration and intensity, I believe that, up to a point, it exists in most people. How far it remains undisturbed depends partly on external circumstances. But the internal factors underlying it – above all the capacity for love – appear to be innate. Destructive impulses, especially strong envy, may at an early stage disturb this particular bond with the mother. If envy of the feeding breast is strong, the full gratification is interfered with because . . . it is characteristic of envy that it implies robbing the object of what it possesses, and spoiling it.
>
> The infant can only experience complete enjoyment if the capacity for love is sufficiently developed; and it is enjoyment that forms the basis for gratitude. Freud described the infant's bliss in being suckled as the prototype of sexual gratification.[2] In my view these experiences constitute not only the basis of sexual gratification but of all later happiness, and make possible the feeling of unity with another person; such unity means being fully understood, which is essential for every happy love relation or friendship. At best, such an understanding needs no words to express it, which demonstrates its derivation from the earliest closeness with the mother in the

preverbal stage. The capacity to enjoy fully the first relation to the breast forms the foundation for experiencing pleasure from various sources.

If the undisturbed enjoyment in being fed is frequently experienced, the introjection of the good breast comes about with relative security. A full gratification at the breast means that the infant feels he has received from his loved object a unique gift which he wants to keep. This is the basis of gratitude.

1 "The Emotional Life of the Infant" (1952).

2 *Three Essays on the Theory of Sexuality.*

[Klein, 1957, p.187]

When this paper is discussed it is usually envy that is treated of and rarely gratitude which therefore has the status of Cinderella before the ball. She has yet to be invested by the fairy godmother, let alone to marry the prince. I think psychoanalysis waits in a state of splitting upon this happy union of envy and gratitude. Similarly, in her paper on schizoid mechanisms, it is Klein's remarks about paranoid apprehension that are regarded and not her remarks about the apprehensions of annihilation that arise from the weakness and undevelopment of the early ego. In this culture of splitting it is only Winnicott (1971) who is allowed to remind us of the consequences for development of the premature loss of infantile omnipotence. In this scenario we read Klein wrongly and selectively. Here, perhaps, she can be, in our projections, only the ugly sister.

In a demonstration supervision at the British Association of Psychotherapists near the turn of the century Donald Meltzer said "If you fall in love with psychoanalysis you have to take what you get". He meant that to undertake psychoanalysis for the purpose of becoming prosperous is wrong. He addressed the thesis that it is therapeutic for patients to pay a fee that makes a significant inroad upon their disposable income with the question: "What do you charge Bill Gates?" He professed that his practice of taking from patients those fees which they assessed themselves as able to afford, within a maximum he specified, was the only proper conduct. I took him to be addressing himself to greed and especially to the denial of greed among practitioners. I took him to intend the mode of moral censure, as an analytic Savonarola. In reply to comments from the

floor he confirmed that, indeed, by this process he would sometimes, but inevitably, be denied his due.

In the vein of retaliatory spite at the supposed greed of the analyst
I have heard a presumably apocryphal tale of Lacan taking his fee in
notes after each session and having by the end of the day a shirt
pocket that crackled with his takings. I assume that in this story the
shirt is made of silk. On the theme of charging what the patient can
afford I remember a patient I worked with in the days when I asked
for a fee determined by means. His response to this way of setting a
fee was to say that he would not subsidise the psychotherapy of
others. Such was his difficulty of making inferences from his associations that it was never possible for us to derive any benefit from
trying to understand this. To this day I am left with feelings divided
between resentment at his meanness and sympathy with the
resentment we feel when siblings get more than we do or have it
easier. As might be expected, the treatment foundered early, perhaps
because it is only now that I can really appreciate the piquancy of
sibling rivalry. I think there is a reciprocal phenomenon for the psychotherapist in the difference in feelings for one patient and for
another which is attributable to the difference in what they pay.
Somewhere I have heard it said that it is therefore essential to
charge each patient the same fee. But most of us could never get a
full practice without low fee patients and for some low fee patients,
with such a system, it might be hard to find psychotherapy at
all. What we can say is that analysts who are in a position to do
this enjoy a factor of consistency and even purity in their work
which is a privilege. This is a matter of the psychotherapist's own
feelings in the transference, not about feelings induced in him by the
client in the countertransference. Many other factors in the client as
well as the fee he pays command feelings in the psychotherapist's
own transference. These feelings are of interest because they
straddle the boundary between the practitioner's supervision and
his analysis.

I remember the late Nina Coltart, at a public lecture at the LCP,
describing her work with a patient whom she diagnosed as having
unlikeability as a symptom of his disturbance rather than an
essential quality of character. What better way to keep people at a
safe distance than to be not very nice? Conversely another patient
once said she lived in dread of the psychotherapist like the one in

Ordinary People, the film directed by Robert Redford in 1980. This psychotherapist, a Daddy figure in a sweater, threw himself metaphorically upon and physically beside his male teenage patient insisting intrusively that he was the young man's friend. This only intensified the young man's schizoid stasis and did not help his struggle to acknowledge a rejecting mother.

Having considered briefly that it may not be love which we charge for, and that love cannot be provided or withheld at will, I would like to return to the question: *what has love become and what kind of love is it we pay for?* Balint, (1968) posits primary love where Klein may be wrongly characterized as exclusively concerned with primary hate. But this primary love is given not by the mother but by the baby. He says that:

> ... offering to the patient a "primary object", of course, is not tantamount to giving primary love; in any case mothers do not *give* it either. What they do is to behave truly as primary objects, that is, to offer themselves as primary objects to be cathected by primary love. This difference between "giving primary love" and "offering oneself to be cathected by primary love" may be of fundamental importance for our technique not only with regressed patients, but also with a number of difficult treatment situations.
>
> To describe the same role from a different angle, i.e. using different "words": the analyst must function during these periods as a provider of time and of milieu. This does not mean that he is under obligation to compensate for the patient's early privations and give more care, love, affection than the patient's parents have given originally (and even if he tried, he would almost certainly fail). What the analyst must provide – and, if at all possible, during the regular sessions only – is sufficient time free from extrinsic temptations, stimuli, and demands, including those originating from himself (the analyst). The aim is that the patient should be able to find himself, to accept himself, and to get on with himself, knowing all the time that there is a scar in himself, his basic fault, which cannot be "analysed" out of existence; moreover, he must be allowed to discover *his* way to the world of objects – and not be shown the "right" way by some profound or correct interpretation. If this can be done, the patient will not feel that the objects impinge on, and oppress, him. It is only to this extent that the analyst should provide a better, more "understanding" environment, but in no other way, in particular not in the form of more care, love, attention, gratification, or protection.

Perhaps it ought to be stressed that considerations of this kind may serve as criteria for deciding whether a certain "craving" or "need" should be satisfied, or recognized but left unsatisfied. [Balint, 1968, p. 179]

Of course the concept of projective identification and the mother's role as container of projections adds something to the idea of "*offering oneself to be cathected by primary love*". It emphasizes how much more love is than strong and particular affection and how closely it relates to hate, here by modifying hateful projections. This does not answer fully the question of what love has become but it does show psychoanalysis coming to a more sophisticated appreciation of it as a function. Bion (1962b, p. 35) specifies this containing function of the mother as reverie, saying: ". . . when the mother loves the infant what does she do with it? Leaving aside the physical channels of communication my impression is that her love is expressed by reverie."

The word reverie with its invocation of the dream and its implication of a dreamy state also suggests Winnicott's (1956) term, primary maternal preoccupation. He also writes of the ordinary devoted mother. This approach has more of the familiar positive sense of love as attachment. It is in his comments on hate and the countertransference (1947) that Winnicott addresses the aspect of love which has to do with hate. So prevalent are anxiety and depression about destructive impulses that it is important to emphasize the function of the mother's love as accommodating hate. But of course what is meant here is the accommodation of the infant's hate. When Winnicott writes of charging for sessions it is of the psychotherapist's own hate he writes.

Finally, there is how much more some patients pay for love than just in fees and how this may have the purpose of neutralizing love in a narcissistic way. Many find it hard to accept a gift if they do not have the means to reciprocate with something of equivalent value, in the ambivalent spirit of the Potlach. We know the feeling of not having sufficient resources to reciprocate. Instead of feeling that one has had something, one feels that in being given anything, the implication of dependency is unbearable Now the purpose of reciprocation is to deny dependency, to deny actually needing what we get. Patients pay psychotherapists in the currency of compliance,

of admiration, of entertainment. We fear that, far from being enter-
taining, we are boring, sometimes because we fear that the other
person must hate and despise our neediness and undevelopment as
much as we do. Here, then, paying may not buy love but buy it off.
Clinically, this is different from paying to compensate the psychotherapist for our hostility. That compensation too might be to deny
in a narcissistic way our dependency upon a container.

Although he died in such disfavour Bhagwan Rajnish has the last
word. He says repeatedly in one of his recorded talks which I heard
in the 1970s: "We are beggars in love. We cannot possibly hope to
deserve love, nor to be able to pay for it. We are given love because
we need it so much. We are beggars in love."

CHAPTER EIGHT

Supervision in a forensic unit: how recycled trauma shapes the container in team supervision[1]

Richard Morgan-Jones

Emotional demands on staff and the management of dissociation

A forensic unit works with patients who have committed crimes while in the grip of mental illness. Crimes committed or attempted include murder, rape, bodily harm, hostage taking and paedophilia. On behalf of society, staff manage the contradiction between society's different expectations. On the one hand their task is to protect the community from dangerous people while on the other they have to treat and rehabilitate them, deciding who is safe to return to the community and when. Supervision needs to address these complex and sometimes contradictory tasks in order to find meaning in the work and to inform their crucial decisions.

Staff who choose to work with such damaged and damaging people take on a huge responsibility on behalf of society. It takes enormous courage on a daily basis to know how dangerous some of the patients can be. This makes for a work group that has to find ways of keeping up their morale and leaving at the end of each working day sufficiently emotionally intact to be able to have a life outside work with friends and family that is not contaminated by the secondary traumatization of intrusive violent thoughts and feelings.

This demands of staff a capacity to dissociate emotionally to be able to survive. I use the term dissociation rather than splitting because it can include the conscious element of disavowal/denial through which unwanted feelings and knowledge are negated. Healthy dissociation can be contrasted with the unhealthy dissociation used by their patients to deal with an overload of mental illness, childhood violence and neglect as a consequence of such accumulated stresses and trauma. It is this unhealthy dissociation that can bring with it sudden and impulsive behaviour with its instant demands for enactment of revenge and aggression that so often leads to violent crimes against the person. It is worth noting how often such crimes performed by patients who are diagnosed as mentally ill attract diagnoses of psychoses, schizophrenia or personality disorder, for which they are treated psychiatrically, when many are suffering from accumulated Post Traumatic Stress Disorder.

There are two sorts of courage in facing dangerous situations. One is the courage that comes of ignoring dangers and many brave deeds are made of that kind of courage. This is dissociated courage. The other is the courage of knowing and thinking about what the risks actually are and acting thoughtfully. It was this second sort of courage that Bion wrote about from his time as an officer in the First World War trenches: "The experienced officer is one who can think while under fire" (Bion, 1986). Working with staff in forensic services over a period of four years, I saw many demonstrations of that sort of courage.

The recycling of traumatic abuse[2]

Clinical story

> Patient A was bought up in a large fatherless family where mother earned her living as a prostitute. As the youngest of six children he was neglected and exposed to the visits of a series of men, sometimes violent, who occasionally stayed with his mother. When his mother became ill and could no longer work, she took to her bed and was looked after by this young boy who also shared her bed and the pain of exposure to an increasingly intrusive skin cancer. Thus as a child

he experienced neglect and insecurity in an impoverished family, and was also compromised by the revulsion he felt towards a mother who sought physical comfort from his young body although he had no memory of genital sexual abuse.

When she died and he was adopted at the age of 10, his initial security eventually brought out the undigested emotional and physical trauma he had experienced as a child and the adoption broke down in adolescence when he tried to seduce his adopted sister. Eventually a foster placement provided him with some security although in his early twenties he found leaving home and achieving independence unbearable. He developed paranoid fantasies about being poisoned by his mother and was arrested, having twice attempted to murder his foster mother with a knife while under the influence of drugs.

He was diagnosed as suffering from paranoid schizophrenia and because of diminished responsibility was sent for treatment to the forensic unit rather than prison. There, while heavily sedated, he presented as a conforming and withdrawn patient who began to show that he could join in physical sporting activities. His medication was reduced and he was considered for a move to the rehabilitation unit within the hospital setting. The week before this move towards greater freedom the social worker, who would be responsible for his eventual care in the community, expressed her anxiety about whether he was ready for this move and reminded colleagues in a case discussion about his former crimes and tendency to violence. In an attempt to ascertain that he was safe for the move, his room was included among those for routine searches with the occupant present, and a flick knife was discovered by a staff nurse. When confronted, A denied knowledge of it, saying it had been planted, and he made a formal complaint against the unit staff for violating his privacy.

He appeared accepting after the hearing at which the psychiatrist suggested he was unwell again, but a week later he violently attacked a staff nurse who had ventured alone into his room for a conversation with him, ignoring the warning in his notes not to be alone with him. She was badly frightened after he held her hostage for an hour. She received minimal de-briefing after this traumatic incident, saying she was all right, only to collapse into inconsolable shaking and tears at work a week later. She was then off sick for three months.

In a supervision session one year after this incident it was possible to begin to talk about this man and his story of repeating trauma in a way that would enable the team to understand something of what had provoked these incidents. It took some time to elicit his story from the records and notes across different agencies including those within the unit. His childhood story, its relation to his index offence, its repetition in symbolic intrusiveness by staff and his violent repeating of the trauma of violation and terrorization could all be seen as versions of past privations in finding and using help to contain the primitive invasions and lack of secure boundaries from childhood. The research done, it was yet another matter to begin to apprise staff across the different shift systems to ways of understanding that might inform their relatedness to him, let alone establish a therapeutic relationship with him that might provide ownership and insight into such a traumatized and traumatizing life story for which reparation and the beginnings of grieving had not begun.

Comment on clinical story

The staff nurse had dissociated from what she knew about how dangerous this patient could be. Her "bravado" was overtly motivated by a wish to normalize relations with the patient. The anxiety about his moving on was expressed by the social worker who carried on behalf of the system the anxiety over the soundness of decisions about rehabilitation and whether the patient would be safe from causing harm. For the patient the intrusiveness of the search was experienced as a repeated version of a familiar intrusiveness that he had experienced at the hands of his mother and which could make him murderous. In the event what he re-enacted was an attack upon a woman that had a sexual element. At the same time he visited upon her his childhood terror of being held as an emotional hostage by and for his mother. It was perhaps a way of trying to get rid of the trauma of feeling unsexed as a child by the way his mother used him as an extension of her own need for physical and emotional comfort.

Unsexing: the relation between dissociated abuse, disordered personality and violence

The clinical narrative above illustrates the need for a word that collectively describes what both men and women have in common as a result of sexual intrusiveness, abuse and loss of boundaries. Freud suggested the word "castration" and yet it is essentially a male word relating to his much criticized theory of castration anxiety as key for women as well as for men (Freud 1905). He connected it to his description of "disavowal", the dynamic in the mind where the person can believe two opposing and contradictory things at the same time and not integrate or see the implications of each to distinguish reality. Freud attached the dynamics of disavowal to the discovery of the difference between the sexes, yet in relation to trauma it has other contexts. Common sense language describes this as "not letting your left hand know what your right hand is doing".

In place of "castration" I would like to suggest instead the older word "unsexed" used by Shakespeare to describe Lady Macbeth's attempts at murderous bravado as she tries to dissociate herself from her feminine identity:

> Come, you spirits
> That tend on mortal thoughts, unsex me here
> And fill me from the crown to the toe top-full
> Of direst cruelty! Make thick my blood,
> Stop up the access and passage to remorse,
> That no compunctious visitings of nature
> Shake my fell purpose nor keep peace between
> The effect and it! Come to my woman's breasts,
> And take my milk for gall, your murthering ministers,
> Wherever in your sightless substances
> You wait on nature's mischief! Come, thick night,
> And pall thee in the dunnest smoke of hell
> That my keen knife see not the wound it makes
> Nor heaven peep through the blanket of the dark
> To cry, "Hold, hold!"
> > Shakespeare: *Macbeth*, I.v, 37–51

This scene expresses conscious psychopathic personality disorder in process. With triumphant omnipotence, conscience and maternal and feminine identity are violently repudiated (Perelberg, 1999). Both men and women are unsexed by abuse and seek, in re-enacting it, to express entitlement to evacuate it into others. They do this to get distance from the trauma sometimes through violent means. This means indulging in the process of self-emptying and dissociation which Lady Macbeth then goes on to conceal behind her sleep walking, disowned guilt and eventual suicide. This in turn represents the dissociated trauma of self/other murder sheltering behind mental illness, not uncommon in forensic work.

Bentovim's model of recycling of trauma

Bentovim (1992) provides an invaluable insight into the nature of families and institutions within which trauma is recycled. Figures 1 and 2 illustrate his attempts to schematize clinical experience of traumatized systems and the powerlessness they engender where there may be sexual and or violent abuse.

The top box of Figure 1 describes the process of repetition of the trauma through triggers that re-stimulate internal ideas and sensations. External events have signalled and triggered the internal vulnerability to re-experiencing an emotionally undigestible trauma. The lower right box describes the persecuting sensations and anxieties that threaten to overwhelm the protective shield that has not been internalized. The lower left box describes the schizoid

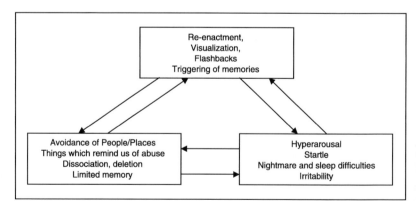

FIGURE 1   Trauma organized systems: traumatic response to sexual or violent abuse (after Bentovim, 2002).

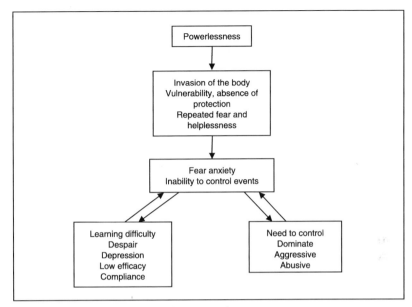

FIGURE 2   Powerlessness (after Bentovim, 2002).

defence with its violent splitting observed in avoidant behaviour and closure of synaptic connections to protect the fragile self from the terrors of annihilation and powerlessness.

Figure 2 explores the consequence of these experiences of power-lessness. The second box down describes the terrors that accompany fears of engulfment that are familiar in sexually overstimulated and abused people as well as those who have been tortured (Morgan-Jones, 2004). The third box down describes the mental state that creates and is added to by threatened loss of control, both internal and external. The lower right box describes the consequent anti-social and aggressive behaviour common in forensic work. The lower left box describes the psychic retreats (Steiner, 1993) resorted to in face of the fears of engaging in retaliatory aggressiveness. This corner also describes the retreated mental illness disability identity behind which narcissistic and aggressive personality disordered criminals can retreat passively to hide their entitlement and guilt about their crimes.

The significance of these figures for staff working in systems of care for violent and traumatized patients is not only that they can have a tool for understanding the extremes of the movement between hyper-arousal, avoidance and re-enactment but also that they provide understanding of the ways in which patients' conscious and unconscious attempts to divest themselves of these experiences can lead staff to unwittingly repeat these experiences, re-traumatizing the patients, themselves or their colleagues. Containing these experiences of patients projecting the bully who is then complained about are central to supervision work.

This was frequently illustrated in supervision sessions where staff reviewed a violent incident. People often felt inhibited in the debriefing from enquiring of colleagues whether they too thought that staff attitudes, disengagement, excitement or provocation might have contributed towards what happened. A common dynamic was the frequently unacknowledged tension between excitement at the danger involved, displayed in bravado attempts to boast prowess at control and restraint techniques on the one hand and avoidance of engagement with patients and their states of mind on the other. The cycle of disengagement of staff leading to boredom and attempts to re-stimulate withdrawn and institutionalized patients could frequently be observed in accounts of experiences of violent incidents.

*Countertransference that led to reflection on
a shared experience*

During regular supervision with groups of staff within the unit there were many opportunities to explore stories about the dangerous nature of the patients. One incident illustrates how this was communicated to me in a way that allowed me to use my countertransference experience to understand anxieties that had to be discharged to be dealt with, rather than thought about. In this example I will use my own experience and reflections.

In order to provide an uninterrupted space away from the work base, one group of supervisors met with me in the training room of the most secure part of the unit where the most dangerous and secluded patients lived. Entrance was via a narrow double locked entry system with reinforced glass doors and a staff observation post that reminded me of the two-hour wait to enter an iron curtain country. I had noticed that this formality was treated jokingly by staff and as a source of routine, especially when there were visitors like myself. No quarter was given to the unexpected fears and apprehensions of an outsider unused to this ritual. During a comfort break I was told that the staff toilet which usually had to be unlocked was out of order, but I could use the toilet in the highly secure medical wing where there were padded rooms with observation spy-holes and secure prison anti-suicide furniture. The joke was made that I might like to be accompanied just in case I was taken hostage. My internal leap of terror took me back to an experience of a university vacation job as a psychiatric nurse where I slept in a room that had been a former padded cell and where I had been assaulted by a stranger entering through the window in the middle of the night. It was then made clear that the speaker was only teasing me, that there was no patient in the secure ward and that I was quite safe. My teaser had been one of the supervisors whom I trusted more than most as he was confiding, self-aware, sensitive, and appropriately protective of himself and of others.

I felt it valuable to reveal my inner reactions which brought with it the shock at what had been visited upon me and an opportunity to explore the range of bravado and fearful reactions that staff had to deal with in themselves on a daily basis in order to do the work. As one person stated: "It's what stops us really thinking about the patients. It's the extreme of terror one moment and the need to put a brave face on it the next. And we live in a culture where we dare not say what we really feel."

This shared experience behind a "joke" and "teasing" provided a chance to reflect on experience and to demonstrate how informal supervision moments can be created. It also provided an opportunity for linking personal experience to group dynamics and the understanding of the task of the unit as a whole in containing conflicting messages of aggression towards and sympathy for violent and violated patients on behalf of a wider society.

Bion's theory of group dynamics

Bion pioneered the understanding of how split-off psychotic anxieties in groups can lead to group behaviour that avoids the work of
thinking and reflecting on experience. These anxieties, he suggests,
provoke basic assumption activity (ba) where the group behaves as
if it has to club together in a certain way to survive (Bion, 1962a). He
suggested three ways groups shaped their dynamics:

1. There was a leader, belief or cause on which to depend (ba-D,
    Dependence);
2. There was a common foe to fight or flee from (ba-F-F, Fight-
    Flight);
3. There was a sense of expectation that a pair in the group would
    resolve all its problems (ba-P, Pairing).

Within the forensic unit the psychotic anxieties of working with
patients capable of unexpected, violent and/or psychotic episodes
creates a climate where consciousness of danger and truth about risk
is painful to think about. This leads to a range of basic assumption
behaviour within the staff team, which often echoes the dynamics of
the patients as individuals or a group.

   Hopper (2003) has pointed out that in his theory of basic assumption group dynamics Bion focused on the psychotic and projective
aspects of groups rather than the introjective or work-effective
dynamics. This last example illustrated the possibility of recruiting
the considerable skill of many staff in being able to articulate their
experience and awareness, demonstrating their capacity to lose the
container, express the contained – projected into me – for what it
was, and share in the process and experience of re-shaping the containing understanding by learning from experience. It showed how
they were able to make the connection between the informal and
hidden insights, making them available to the more public arena of
supervision for clarification through reflection and thought via a
shared experience of which I had been the butt!

Me-ness as a basic assumption

In addition to the examples above I have noticed that staff move between two states of mind. One is highly professional and experienced thoughtful team consideration and assessment of the risks individual patients pose. The other is the avoidance of mutual inter-dependence in refusing to acknowledge the need for reliable backup in risky situations. Portable emergency communicators were not always checked to be sure they were in working order before staff entered potentially dangerous situations and occasionally staff carried out lone observations of psychotic patients while knowing that they were meant to do this in pairs. The need for ordinary inter-dependence was sometimes hard to acknowledge, especially in a shift system where people had little choice over who their colleagues were and team formation was not always acknowledged as an important exercise.

At times it seemed as if the shift groups were avoiding the need even to be a group at all, illustrating avoidance of inter-dependency, enhancing the "each-man-for-himself" culture and exemplifying what Lawrence, Bain and Gould described as a basic assumption group of "me-ness" (Lawrence, Bain & Gould, 2000). They describe avoidance of group belonging, group existence and group boundaries as one response to the painfulness and anxieties stirred by the unpredictable unknowns of how colleagues work and what patients may provoke. From a cultural perspective this dynamic describes what Christopher Lasch called the "Culture of Narcissism" (Lasch, 1979).

Developments in psychoanalytic understanding of extremes of trauma, neglect and abuse and the resultant narcissistic wounds

Psychoanalytic understanding of narcissistic personality disorders sheds new insight into its origins, defensive structures and ways to intervene clinically. Winnicott writes of the psychological impingements in infancy before the child has developed sufficient ego strength to deal with this (Winnicott, 1963). A range of writers have described primitive defences of the self which appear to take one of two forms: either they are stupefying, crustaceous and shell-like or they are hypersensitive, boundary-less, fluid and jelly-like (Tustin, 1981, Hopper, 2003, Symington, 2002). In these ways people desperately attempt to defend themselves against annihilation or the traumatic invasiveness of sexual or violent overexcitement or trauma which cannot be digested. The effects of such narcissistic wounds have been charted by Bateman, drawing on Rosenfeld's outline of different technique with thin- and thick-skinned narcissism (Bateman, 1998). Likewise Steiner provides an invaluable map of the narcissistic personality organization with all its personality disordered aspects of "revenge, resentment, remorse and reparation" (Steiner, 1993).

Mitrani has noted the way in which people use extra-ordinary protections of self-harm, self-stupefaction and self-mortification in order to deal with primitive terrors and keep at bay fragmented corners of the personality that do function, lest they be destroyed by the rest (Mitrani, 2002). These personality features confirm Bion's notion that psychosis is not the absence of reality and relatedness but an active and destructive attack upon it, found persistently in disordered personalities (Bion, 1967).

Doctor and others who have worked with a psychoanalytic approach within the forensic system have made invaluable contributions to the difficult task of assessing risk in patients who may be violent to themselves, others or their children (Doctor, 2003). One key development is the work of Welldon (1992) at the Portman Clinic in describing the shock and therefore denial at the nature and frequency of abuse at the hands not of men and fathers but of mothers. Motz (2001) provides an excellent summary of her work as a forensic psychologist in assessing the safety of mothers and children. She spells out the significance, meaning and origins of maternal murder, sexual and violent abuse of children and of Munchausen's disease by proxy. A similar finding is echoed by Sinason's work on abuse of those with learning difficulties, and those who have been ritually abused where mothers take a key role in the abuse (Sinason, 1994).

Meltzer links Bion's theories on group behaviour with his work on psychoanalysis suggesting that sense stimuli (beta-elements) that are uncontained by maternal reverie (alpha-function) cause regression to *"group mentality and its near ally somatic innervation"* (Meltzer, 1986, p. 35, original emphasis) in group and organizational dynamics. The consequences can be psychosomatic states, mindless hallucination or evacuating violence. This is highly relevant to the clinical data on forensic patients described in this paper and to the way trauma is recycled, described by Bentovim (see Figures 1 and 2 above).

Hopper's version of a fourth basic assumption

Incohesion: aggregation/massification or (ba- I:A/M)

Expanding on Bion's proto-mental system (beta-elements), Hopper has described the encapsulated way in which traumatized experiences within the personality are put beyond reach by fusion with others or by fission within the self. To put it in terms of the traumatized individual, sexually or violently abused children often develop the capacity to consciously or unconsciously distance themselves from their own bodily and emotional experience in order to survive the overload of annihilating bombarding sensations and cognitive dissonance. This can create an encapsulated internal and dissociated corner of the self that is avoided at all costs for fear that it will engulf and swallow up a person's fragile identity. This becomes the source of unthinkable terror that is shunned or visited upon others and this provides insight into the disordered personality of the mentally ill criminal and the borderline person terrified by fear of madness or by mad-driving inner voices.

Hopper develops Bion's theory of group functioning and basic assumption activity, where traumatized individuals can personify or collectively behave within a desperate illusion of solidarity. He defines two constellations to be found in groups where extreme trauma is a feature. To do this he provides an appreciation and a critique of Turquet's (1975) extension of Bion's theory into a fourth basic assumption using the theme of "Oneness" (ba-O) and a fusion with a uniform identity rather than the individual managing the primitive anxieties of being out of step. He also provides an appreciation and a criticism of Lawrence, Bain and Gould's (2000) fifth basic assumption of "me-ness" (ba-M), based on the experience of fission or splitting into an individuality that tries to know no restriction from the group or the reality of its boundaries (cf. Cano, 1998).

Hopper's analysis takes these theories further and integrates them into a unified theory of "incohesion". Incohesion, he suggests, contrasts the experience of oneness and fusion and what he calls massification on the one hand with that of fission, splitting and what he calls aggregation on the other. Aggregation, he suggests, is undifferentiated normlessness, fragmentation, mindlessness, capacity for violent acting and sadistic scapegoating.

Massification, he suggests, is subservience to a dominant limiting culture that is uniform in dress, language, behaviour and loss of individuality. Both have the characteristic of war on meaning and thoughtful exchange or any sign of individuality. A psychiatrist describes a sub-group of female forensic patients "They are round and overweight, shaven headed and dressed . . . colourlessly" (Zachary, 2004). This is an example of massification. Such groupings can be seen as signs of unsexing through trauma and abuse and the search for an identity in a commonality of incoherent avoidance. Hopper also suggests that it is fear of annihilation that is more primitive than the analysis of envy and the death instinct. Thereby he aims to move Bion's and Turquet's basic assumption theories beyond the confines of their Kleinian heritage.

Team supervision and group dynamics

One of the aims of regular supervision within work groups is to help staff to express and observe the way their dynamics are shaped by projected experiences and tensions within and between patients. This detoxification process relies on an understanding of projective identification as a process. Unwanted experience within patients can be projected into staff who then unconsciously identify with it in their attitudes and behaviour, expressing something on behalf of the patient. In short this describes psychotic processes in which professional's lose part of their minds. As Hopper puts it:

> The term "psychotic" is being used to mean a diminution of effective contact with reality. There is a group mentality that has such a culture that the individual, despite his or her sophisticated and mature skills, can be caused to regress to and be temporarily caught up in primitive splitting and projective identification, depersonalisation, and infantile regression. [Hopper, 2003 p. 30]

To be able to do this work the team is at the mercy of members' ability to reveal their true thoughts and feelings and to work them through with colleagues in a way that identifies the source of tensions within the team. A typical example is in case discussion where one staff person appears very protective about a patient's vulnerability while another has a feeling of hatred and revulsion at the horror of a crime that was committed for which there has been no sign of remorse let alone contrition. Each member of staff picks up a different aspect of the patient's inability to integrate early and current experiences of neglect and abuse and vulnerability on the one hand along with experiences of appropriate shame and victim empathy on the other. Together the staff can reconstruct a narrative about the patient. They are the better resourced to help the patient to begin the task of some integration that can include the experience of remorse, grief and loss.

This work depends upon the integrity of the staff team in being able to acknowledge lost and split off parts of their own identifications with patients. The staff need to oscillate between a psychotic mentality that can pick up and receive messages about patients and a mature work group and professional mentality that can understand and use these comprehensions. This sophisticated oscillation is invaluable to the work and builds the morale of the therapeutic team. In this sense the building of a group supervision container can be shaped by the nature of the experiences of fielding the threats of recycling trauma. As I understand it this was what was meant by Bion's analogy of the container contained, where the container is shaped by the nature of the experiences searching for a mate in understanding and role responsiveness (Bion, 1963).

An unusual example of making sense of good containment within part of the existing rehabilitation programme was offered during a team supervision session where a DIY group was discussed and its meaning for the patient group explored.

The DIY group

The DIY group was designed to enhance independent living skills and group co-operation. Members were rewarded with pay and had a say in designing how tasks were done with the chance to share skills, support each other and to develop new skills.

In discussing the effects of the group in team supervision we could see a particular dynamic. In planning and reviewing their work together patients were enabled to experience interdependence and the manageable consequences of ordinary let down and un-reliability, contrasting with the drastic failed dependency of their family relations. Within the context of reparative work (internal redecoration) they were able to talk side by side in a way that enabled deeper sharing and exploration of experience than could ever have been possible in a face-to-face therapy group where forensic patients so often feel under the spotlight searching for how they can be assessed to move towards or defend against moves towards greater social movement and freedom beyond the unit. In exploring these meanings staff were able to shape the group experience towards providing interactions through shared work that would relate to needed developments in individuals. Insights and metaphors could be developed with patients from the decorating tasks, within a safe and contained work task. Occupational therapy was benefited and informed by psychodynamic understandings while the staff increased their confidence in their skill in doing the right things intuitively to provide an effective experience that was both rehabilitative and therapeutic.

Sexual acting out by a staff member: its meaning and repercussions

One of the clearest examples of these group dynamics was expressed in an incident that shocked and surprised most members of staff who knew about it. A junior staff member began a sexual affair with one of the patients in another part of the hospital. Staff on that unit turned a blind eye to increasingly frequent visits when the two were alone, under the guise of a professional assessment task, even though many later said they had known what was going on between them. When the affair was revealed the staff member was suspended and sacked after a disciplinary hearing.

The effect of this event on staff was profound. Nearest colleagues had experienced a reliable, supportive and insightful colleague who believed in the importance of boundaries in relation to patients who had had theirs breached.

Some of the staff were shocked and surprised; some were blasé. In consequence there was the conflict of both protest and acquiescence to management deciding to continue to work with this individual who continued in the unit. Indeed the suspended staff member was allowed to continue to visit the patient on the ward after the suspension.

Such an extreme example of the disavowal and dissociation of a part of the self in a professional, that suddenly returns to take over what had come to be trustworthy, is a kind of breakdown. It provides a sign of the problems of dissociation that has to be managed by all who undertake this work. It suggests how much colleagues are reliant upon each other for their mental health and maturity to manage their personal lives in a way that does not impinge on their professional lives. In this case a sense of entitlement and opportunism to use a position of authority to secure intimacy with a sectioned patient dismissed the need to explore and contain such issues in supervision, which was also being attacked. What got acted out was an unresolved engagement with violated and damaged relationships that undermined a professional role and the trust of colleagues and patients in staff generally.

My task of consulting to the staff team through the subsequent experiences of loss and betrayal was complicated. In trying to make sense of these events it was clear that the growing awareness of this developing intimacy among a wider group of staff on the other unit and the access that had been allowed subsequent to suspension, were acts of denial of the true meaning of what damage had been done to the work of the unit, the morale of staff and to the long-term security of one patient.

In piecing together understandings we were able to understand the suspended staff member as someone who represented wider issues within the dynamics of the staff group, including as a representative of the erotic stimulation of violence and trauma that was a characteristic of failed dependency in the lives of many patients. The capacity to face competing explanations expressed a competence at moving between person, role and system that had been at the core of the supervision project.

The exploitation of a patient provided an opportunity to revisit ethical issues and to explore the variety of feelings that staff had about the ethical framework within which they worked as professionals in a way that gave ethics a meaning and themselves a professional identity. The expression of what had been a symbolically incestuous act by someone in a caring and therefore a quasi-parental role, brought home the reality of the abuse that many patients had experienced at the hands of their caretakers. Colleagues experienced for themselves the shock of feeling betrayed, their trust abused and the tragedy of losing someone whom they had experienced as a good friend and colleague.

The event seemed to confirm a group dynamic in which entitlement to intimacy, at whatever price, was a just return for doing such an emotionally demanding job. People were thereby aggregated as individuals rather than as differentiated patients and staff, and all were perceived to have an equal right to "happiness" and intimacy.

It is possible to see this piece of acting out as an example of collusion over the group dynamic of a shared basic assumption of the need for there to be a pair who would prove that love was possible within a climate of violence, abuse and trauma (Bion's baP). I believe that there is evidence to suggest that Hopper's development of Turquet's and Lawrence's basic assumption theories into a clear combined fourth basic assumption of "incoherence" as a development of Bion's theory of group mentality. This was expressed in the incoherent, shocked and denying reaction of management and staff to this incident and its meanings. While individuals and pairs clearly and courageously owned to knowing, understanding and even coming to terms with the appalling breach of ethics that had taken place, there was no context in which this attitude and learning was made available coherently in order to mend the attack on the worth of the system and its work. This I believe suggests the value in Hopper's theory of group incoherence to develop Bion's theories of the three basic assumption activities that create illusions of group coherence by adding the fourth that describes incoherence.

Conclusion

In responding to the task of addressing the supervision needs of this particular staff group it soon became clear that it was not possible only to focus on relatedness to transference and countertransference issues with clients. The nature of the patients' traumatized backgrounds and the complexity of the institutional task meant that the supervision had to be shaped around the way trauma could be recycled within the staff group as well as in the way staff related to patients.

This paper has tried to illustrate and describe the emotional and physical risks to staff of being secondarily re-traumatized within their work with violated and violating forensic patients. The oscillation between schizoid withdrawal and excitement that may have a sexual element has been tracked. The examples given have suggested that supervision can provide a space where group dynamics can be experienced as reflecting the trauma of patients and their groups. They have also explored the ways in which the institution and its staff has a hand in some of the re-traumatizing processes. It is worth noting that the health and safety of staff and patients alike may depend upon adequate supervision as indeed may the health and safety of the public in the decisions that are made about dangerous patients being rehabilitated.

Notes

1. A version of this paper was given to the Opus (Organisation for the Promotion of an Understanding of Society) Conference 2004.
   A companion paper has been submitted to the Opus journal *Organisation and Society* with more detailed analysis of the organizational development intervention.
2. In order to protect confidentiality incidents are a composition of a number of events.

REFERENCES

Alayarian, A. (2002). Personal communication.

Aymer, C. (2001). Black professionals in white organizations. In: R. Winter & C. Munn-Giddings (Eds.), *A Handbook for Action Research in Health and Social Care* (pp. 131–144). London and New York: Routledge.

Balint, M. (1968). The unobtrusive analyst. In: M. Balint, *The Basic Fault* (p. 179). London: Tavistock Publications.

Barbanel, L. (1980). The therapist's pregnancy. In: B.L. Blum (Ed.), *Psychological Aspects of Pregnancy, Birthing and Bonding* (pp. 232–246). New York: Human Sciences Press.

Bateman, A. (1998). Thick- and thin-skinned organisations and enactment in borderline and narcissistic disorders. *International Journal of Psychoanalysis*, 79: 13–25.

Beattie, J., & Middleton, J. (Eds.) (1969). *Spirit Mediumship and Society in Africa*. London: Routledge & Kegan Paul.

Bentovim, A. (1992). *Trauma-organised Systems: Physical and Sexual Abuse in Families*. London: Karnac Books.

Bentovim, A. (2002). Dissociative Identity Disorder: a developmental perspective. In: V. Sinason (Ed.), *Attachment, Trauma and Multiplicity – Working with Dissociative Identity Disorder*. London: Routledge.

Bernardi, R., & Nieto, M. (1992). What makes the training analysis "good enough"? *International Review of Psycho-Analysis, 19*: 137.

Bibring, G.L. (1959). A study of the psychological processes in pregnancy. *Psychoanalytic Study of the Child, 14*: 115–121.

Bion, W.R. (1962a). *Experiences in Groups*. London: Tavistock.

Bion, W.R. (1962b). *Learning from Experience*. Ch. 9, p.35. London: Heinemann, 1967 [reprinted London: Karnac, 1984].

Bion, Wilfred (1962c). *Learning from Experience*. Ch.28, p.97, para. 9. London: Heinemann [reprinted London: Karnac, 1984].

Bion, W.R. (1963). *Elements of Psycho-Analysis*. London: Karnac Books.

Bion, W.R. (1967). *Second Thoughts*. London: Heinemann.

Bion, W.R. (1970). *Attention and Interpretation*. London: Tavistock [reprinted London: Karnac, 1984].

Bion, W.R. (1986). *The Long Week-End*. London: Free Association Books.

Birkstead-Breen, D. (1986). The experience of having a baby: a developmental view. *Free Associations, 4*: 22–35.

Bollas, C. (1987). *The Shadow of the Object: Psychoanalysis of the Unknown Thought*. London: Free Association Books.

Bott Spillius, E. (Ed.) (1988). *Melanie Klein Today. Developments in Theory and Practice, Volume 1: Mainly Theory*. London: Routledge.

Breen, D. (1977). Some differences between group and individual therapy in connection with the therapist's pregnancy. *International Journal of Group Psychotherapy, 27*: 499–506.

Brewin, C.R. (2003). *Post-traumatic Stress Disorder: Malady or Myth?* London: Yale UP.

Britton, R. (1989). The missing link: parental sexuality in the Oedipus complex. In: J. Steiner (Ed.), *The Oedipus Complex Today. Clinical Implications* (pp. 83–101). London: Karnac.

Britton, R. (1998). *Belief and Imagination: Explorations in Psychoanalysis*. London: Routledge.

Bryan, A., & Aymer, C. (1996). Black social work students and practitioners: survival strategies. *Journal of Social Work Practice, 10*: 113–117.

Cano, D. H. (1998). Oneness and Me-ness in the baG? In: P. Bion, P. Talamo, F. Borgogno & S. Merciai (Eds.), *Bion's Legacy to Groups. Selected Contributions from the International Centennial Conference on the Work of W.R. Bion* (pp. 83–94). London: Karnac.

Casement, P. (1985). *On Learning from the Patient*. London: Free Association Books.

Clementel-Jones, C. (1985). The pregnant psychotherapist's experience:

colleagues' and patients' reactions to the author's first pregnancy. *British Journal of Psychotherapy,* 2: 79–94.

Dalal, F. (1988). The racism of Jung. *Race & Class,* Volume XXIX, Number 3, Institute of Race Relations.

Davids, F. (1988). Two accounts of the management of racial difference in psychotherapy. *Journal of Social Work Practice,* 3(3): 40–51.

Davids, M. F. (1992). The cutting edge of racism: an object relations view. *Bulletin of the British Psychoanalytical Society,* 28: 19–29.

Davids, M. F. (1998). "Internal Racism: A Psychodynamic Perspective on Working with Cultural Difference". The 1998 Lionel Monteith Lecture. Lincoln Centre & Clinic for Psychotherapy. Unpublished.

Deben-Mager, M. (1993). Acting out and transference themes induced by successive pregnancies of the analyst. *International Journal of Psychoanalysis,* 74: 129–139.

Dickinson, H. (2001). The Peppered Moth. *Journal Auto/Biography,* 9 (1 & 2).

Doctor, R. (Ed.) (2003). *Dangerous Patients: A Psychodynamic Approach to Risk Assessment and Management.* London: Karnac.

Drabble, M. (2000). *The Peppered Moth.* London: Viking.

Durban, J., Lazar, R., & Ofer, G. (1993). The Cracked Container, the containing Crack: chronic illness – its effect on the therapist and the therapeutic process. *International Journal of Psychoanalysis,* 74.

Eliade, M. (1982). *Shamanism: Archaic Techniques of Ecstasy.* London: Routledge & Kegan Paul.

Etchegoyen, A. (1993). The analyst's pregnancy and its consequences on her work. *International Journal of Psychoanalysis,* 74: 141–149.

Evans Holmes, D. (1992). Race and transference in psychoanalysis and psychotherapy. *International Journal of Psychoanalysis,* 73: 1.

Fenster, S., Phillips, S.B., & Rapoport, E.R.G. (1986). *The Therapist's Pregnancy-Intrusion in the Analytic Space.* New Jersey: The Analytic Press.

Foster, A. (2001). The duty to care and the need to split. *Journal of Social Work Practice,* 15: 81–90.

Freud, S. (1905, trans 1953). *Three Essays on Sexuality. S.E.,* 7, pp. 123–245 [reprinted in Pelican edition, 1977, vol.7, p. 113ff].

Freud, S. (1913). Totem and taboo: some points of agreement between the mental lives of savages and neurotics. In: S. Freud, Volume 13, *The Origins of Religion: Totem and Taboo, Moses and Monotheism and Other Works.* London: Penguin.

Freud, S. (1919). *Introduction to Psychoanalysis and the War Neuroses, S.E.,* 17, pp. 208–9.

Freud, S. (1920). *Beyond the Pleasure Principle, S.E., 18,* p. 29.

Freud, S. (1924). The loss of reality in neurosis and psychosis. In: *On Psychopathology.* The Pelican Freud Library, vol. 10. London: Penguin.

Freud, S. (1926). *Inhibitions, Symptoms and Anxiety, S.E., 20,* pp. 166–168.

Freud, S. (1927). *Fetishism, S.E., 21,* p. 156.

Garner, H.L. (2003). Making connections: developing racially and culturally sensitive psychoanalytic psychotherapy in NHS psychotherapy departments. *British Journal of Psychotherapy, 19*(4): 503–514.

Gilroy, P., Solomos, J., Findlay, B., & Jones, S. (Eds.) (1982). The organic crisis of British capitalism and race: the experience of the seventies. In: *The Empire Strikes Back: Race and Racism in 70s Britain.* London: Hutchinson, for the Centre for Contemporary Cultural Studies.

Gordon, P. (1993). Keeping therapy white? Psychotherapy trainings and equal opportunities. *British Journal of Psychotherapy, 10*(1): 44–49.

Gottlieb, S. (1989). The pregnant therapist: a potent transference stimulus. *British Journal of Psychotherapy, 5*: 287–299.

Hall, G.S. (1904). *Adolescence: Its Psychology and its Relations to Physiology, Anthropology, Sociology, Sex, Crime, Religion and Education, vol. II.* New York: Appleton.

Haupt, P., & Malcolm. C. (2000). Between hell and hope: an organizational case study of the Truth and Reconciliation Commission (TRC) in South Africa. *Organisational and Social Dynamics, 1*: 113–129.

Hobson, R.E. (1985). *Forms of Feeling: The Heart of Psychotherapy.* London: Routledge.

Hoggett, P. (1998). The internal establishment. In: W.R. Bion, P. Talamo & P. Hoggett (Eds.), *Bion's Legacy to Groups* (pp. 9–24). London: Karnac.

Hopper, E. (2003). *Traumatic Experience in the Unconscious Life of Groups.* London: Jessica Kingsley.

Jones, D. (2001). Shame, disgust, anger and revenge: hand countertransference. *British Journal of Psychotherapy, 17*: 493–504.

Jung, C.G. (1939a [1960]). *The Symbolic Life: Miscellaneous Writings.* Collected Works, vol. 18. London: Routledge and Kegan Paul.

Jung, C.G. (1939b [1960]). *The dreamlike world of India.* Collected Works, vol. 10. London: Routledge and Kegan Paul.

Jung, C.G. (1963). *Memories, Dreams, Reflections.* London: Collins.

Kareem, J. (1992). The Nafsiyat Intercultural Therapy Centre: ideas and experiences in intercultural therapy. In: J. Kareem & R. Littlewood (Eds), *Intercultural Therapy.* London: Blackwell.

Kareem, J., & Littlewood, R. (Eds.) (1992). *Intercultural Therapy*. London: Blackwell.

Klein, M. (1957 [1977]). Envy and Gratitude. In: *Envy and Gratitude and Other Works*. New York: Delta Books.

Klein, M. (1988). *Envy and Gratitude and Other Works 1946–1963*. London: Virago Press.

Kuhn, A. (1995). *Family Secrets. Acts of Meaning and Imagination*. London: Verso.

Langs, R. (1981). The therapeutic relationship and deviations in technique. In: R. Langs (Ed.), *Classics in Psychoanalytic Technique* (pp. 469–488). London: Jason Aronson.

Lasch, C. (1979). *The Culture of Narcissism*. London: Abacus.

Lasky, R. (1990). Catastrophic illness in the analyst and the analyst's emotional reactions to it. *International Journal of Psychoanalysis, 71*: 455–473.

Lawrence, W.G., Bain, A. and Gould, L.J. (1966). The fifth basic assumption. *Free Associations, 6*(1): No. 37.

Lawrence, W.G. (with Bain & Gould) (2000). The fifth basic assumption. In: W.G. Lawrence (2003). *Tongued with Fire*. London: Karnac.

Lax, R.F. (1969). Some considerations about transference and counter-transference manifestations evoked by the therapist's pregnancy. *International Journal of Psychoanalysis, 50*: 363–372.

Littlewood, R., & Lipsedge, M. (1982). *Aliens and Alienists: Ethnic Minorities and Psychiatry*. Harmondsworth: Penguin.

Long, S. (2002). Organisational destructivity and the perverse state of mind. *Organisational and Social Dynamics, 2*: 179–207.

Lorenz, K. (1963 [1967]). *On Aggression*. London: University Paperback.

Macpherson, W. (1999). *The Stephen Lawrence Inquiry: Report of an Inquiry by Sir William Macpherson of Cluny*. London: HM Stationery Office.

Mariotti, P. (1993). The analyst's pregnancy: the patient, the analyst and the space of the unknown. *International Journal of Psychoanalysis, 74*: 151–164.

Meltzer, D. (1986). *Studies in Extended Metapsychology*. Perthshire: The Clunie Press.

Meltzer, D. (1992). *The Claustrum: An Investigation of Claustrophobic Phenomena*. Perthshire: The Clunie Press.

Mendoza, S. (2001). Genital and phallic homosexuality. In: C. Harding (Ed.), *Sexuality: Psychoanalytic Perspectives* (pp. 153–169). Hove: Brunner-Routledge.

Mental Health Foundation (1999). *The Fundamental Facts: All the Latest*

Facts and Figures on Mental Illness. London: The Mental Health Foundation.

Mitrani, J. (2002). *Ordinary People and Extra-ordinary Protections*. London: Routledge.

Mollon, P. (1998). *Multiple Selves, Multiple Voices: Working with Trauma, Violence and Dissociation*. Chichester: Wiley.

Mollon, P. (2002). *Shame and Jealousy: The Hidden Turmoils*. London: Karnac.

Money-Kyrle, R. (1956 [1978]). Normal counter-transference and some of its deviations. In: *The Collected Papers of Roger Money-Kyrle* (pp. 330–342). Perthshire: Clunie Press.

Money-Kyrle, R. (1971 [1978]). The aim of psychoanalysis. In: *The Collected Papers of Roger Money-Kyrle* (pp. 442–449). Perthshire: Clunie Press.

Morgan, H. (1998). Between fear and blindness: the white therapist and the black patient. *Journal of the British Association of Psychotherapists*, 3(1): 48–61.

Morgan-Jones, R.J. (2004). "Taming the fires of Hell: seeking containment for self-destructive defences against the persecutory and depressive agonies of a tortured patient with severe risk of suicide." Unpublished paper given to London Centre for Psychotherapy, Association for Group and Individual Psychotherapy, Brighton Association of Analytic Psychotherapists and staff at the Henderson Hospital.

Motz, A. (2001). *The Psychology of Female Violence*. London: Brunner-Routledge.

NIMHE (National Institute for Mental Health in England) (2003). *Inside Outside: Improving Mental Health Services for Black and Minority Ethnic Communities in England*. London: Department of Health.

Okri, B. (1996). *Birds of Heaven*. London: Phoenix Books.

O' Shaughnessy, E. (1981). A clinical study of a defensive organisation. *International Journal of Psycho-Analysis*, 62: 359–369.

Panksepp, J. (1998). *Affective Neuroscience*. Oxford: OUP.

Papadopoulos, R. (2002). *Therapeutic Care for Refugees*. London: Karnac.

Perelberg, R.J. (1999). The interplay of identifications: violence, hysteria, and the repudiation of femininity. In: G. Kohon (Ed.), *The Dead Mother: The Work of Andre Green*. London: Routledge.

Pines, D. (1972). Pregnancy and motherhood: interaction between fantasy and reality. *British Journal of Medical Psychology*, 45: 333–343.

Pines, D. (1982). The relevance of early psychic development to pregnancy and abortion. *International Journal of Psycho-Analysis*, 63: 311–319.

Raphael-Leff, J. (1980). Psychotherapy with pregnant women. In: B. Blum (Ed.), *Psychological Aspects of Pregnancy, Birthing and Bonding* (pp. 174–205). New York: Human Sciences Press.

Raphael-Leff, J. (1986). Facilitators and regulators: conscious and unconscious processes in pregnancy and early motherhood. *British Journal of Medical Psychology*, 59: 43–55.

Raphael-Leff, J. (1993). *Pregnancy: The Inside Story*. London: Karnac.

Rosenfeld, H. (1987). Some therapeutic and anti-therapeutic factors in the functioning of the analyst. In: H. Rosenfeld, *Impasse and Interpretation* (pp. 31–44). London: Tavistock.

Runnymede Trust. (2000). *The Future of Multi-ethnic Britain: The Report of the Commission on the Future of Multi-ethnic Britain*. London: Profile Books.

Rustin, M.J. (1991). *The Good Society and the Inner World. Psychoanalysis, Politics and Culture*. London: Verso.

Rycroft, C. (1968). *A Critical Dictionary of Psychoanalysis*. Harmonds-worth: Penguin.

Saporta, J. (2003). Synthesizing psychoanalytic and biological approaches to trauma. *Neuro-psychoanalysis*, 5: 98–9, 102, 103.

Scott Peck, M. (1978 [1990]). *The Road Less Travelled*. London: Arrow Books.

Segal. H. (1997). Uses and abuses of counter-transference. In: H. Segal, *Psychoanalysis, Literature and War* (pp. 111–119). London: Routledge.

Sinason, V. (Ed.) (1994). *Treating Survivors of Satanist Abuse*. London: Routledge.

Sinason, V. (Ed.) (2002). *Attachment, Trauma and Multiplicity: Working with Dissociative Identity Disorder*. London: Routledge.

Sontag, S. (1978). *Illness as Metaphor*. New York: Farrar, Straus and Giroux.

Steiner, J. (1993). *Psychic Retreats*. London: Routledge.

Steiner, J. (1987). The interplay between pathological organizations and the paranoid-schizoid and depressive positions. *International Journal of Psychoanalysis*, 68: 69–80.

Steiner, J. (1993). *Psychic Retreats*. London: Routledge.

Symington, N. (2002). *A Pattern of Madness*. London: Karnac.

Tan, R. (1993). Racism and similarity: paranoid-schizoid structures. *British Journal of Psychotherapy*, 10(1): 33–43.

Temperley, J. (1993). Is the Oedipus complex bad news for women? *Free Associations*, 4: 265–275. [Reprinted in: J. Raphael-Leff & R.J. Perelberg (Eds.), 1997, *Female Experience. Three Generations of British Women Psychoanalysts on Work with Women*. London: Routledge.

Thomas, L. (1992). Racism and psychotherapy: working with racism in the consulting room: an analytic view. In: J. Kareem, & R. Littlewood (Eds.), *Intercultural Therapy*. London: Blackwell.

Thomas, L. (2003). Personal communication.

Timimi, S.B. (1996). Race and colour in internal and external reality. *British Journal of Psychotherapy*, 13(2): 183–192.

Treacher, A., & Foster, A. (2004). Regarding difference: respecting others. *Organisational and Social Dynamics*, 4(2): 311–24.

Turquet, P. (1974) Leadership: The individual and the group. In: G.S. Gibbard, J.J. Hartmann, & R.D. Mann (Eds.), *Analysis of Groups*, pp. 87–144. San Francisco: Josey-Bass.

Turquet, P. (1975). Threats to identity in the large group. In: L. Kreeger (Ed.), *The Large Group: Dynamics and Therapy*. London: Constable.

Tustin, F. (1981). *Autistic States in Children*. Hove: Routledge.

Wedderkopp, A. (1990). The therapist's pregnancy: evocative intrusion. *Psychoanalytic Psychotherapy*, 5: 37–58.

Weiss, S. (1975). The effect on the transference of special events occurring during psychoanalysis. *International Journal of Psychoanalysis*, 56: 69–75.

Welldon, E. (1992). *Mother, Madonna, Whore*. London: Free Association Books.

Western, S. (1999). Where's Daddy? Integrating the Paternal Metaphor within the Maternal: The Tavistock tradition of Organizational thinking. Paper presented at the International Society for the Psychoanalytic Study of Organizations Symposium, Toronto. http://www.sba.oakland.edu/ispso/html/1999Symposium/ Western1999a.htm

Winnicott, D.W. (1963). *Fear of Breakdown* [Reprinted in D.W. Winnicott, 1989, *Psychoanalytic Explorations*. London: Karnac].

Winnicott, D.W. (1947 [1975]). Hate in the countertransference. In: D.W. Winnicott, *Through Paediatrics to Psychoanalysis* (pp. 194–203). London: Hogarth Press.

Winnicott, D.W. (1956 [1975]). Primary maternal preoccupation. In: D.W. Winnicott, *Through Paediatrics to Psychoanalysis* (pp. 300–305). London: Hogarth Press.

Winnicott, D.W. (1963 [1965]). The development of the capacity for concern. In: *The Maturational Processes and The Facilitating Environment* (pp. 73–82). London: Hogarth Press.

Winnicott, D.W. (1971). *Playing and Reality*. London: Tavistock Publications [reprinted Harmondsworth: Penguin, 1974].

Winnicott, D.W. (1974). Fear of breakdown. *International Review of Psychoanalysis*, 1: 103–107. Also in: G. Kohon (Ed.), *The British School of Psychoanalysis* (p. 173). London: Free Association Books, 1986.

Winnicott, D.W. (1988a). *Babies and their Mothers*. London: Free Association Books.

Winnicott, D.W. (1988b). *Human Nature*. London: Free Association Books.

Young, R.M. (1994). *Mental Space*. London: Process Press.

Zachary, A. (2001). Uneasy triangles: brief overview of the history of homosexuality. *British Journal of Psychotherapy*, 17: 489–492.

Zachary, A. (2004). Personal communication.

INDEX

Printed in Great Britain
by Amazon

64925978R00102